ISSN 2475-2061

Dediu Newsletter

Author: Michael M. Dediu

I0040933

World Monthly Report
News and Suggestions for Sustainable
Peace, Freedom and Prosperity

Vol. 4, Nr. 6 (42), 6 May 2020

DERC Publishing House
Nashua, New Hampshire, U. S. A.
For subscriptions please use the contact form at www.derc.com

Copyright ©2020 by Michael M. Dediu

All rights reserved

Published and printed in the
United States of America
On the Great Seal of the United States are included:
E Pluribus Unum (Out of many, one)
Annuit Coeptis (He has approved of the undertakings)
Novus Ordo Seclorum (New order of the ages)

Dediu, Michael M.

Dediu Newsletter Vol 4, Number 6 (42), 6 May 2020
World Monthly Report with news and suggestions for
Sustainable Peace, Freedom and Prosperity

ISSN 2475-2061
ISBN 978-1-950999-13-2

Preface

Today there are many more bureaucrats in the world than doctors, but all people want many more doctors, and no bureaucrats!

Patients obviously need doctors, not bureaucrats.

Health care also needs freedom to focus on medical issues, no waste time on bureaucracy. A Global Innovation Research Institute is needed to work on global medical problems.

From a world sustainable peace, good health, freedom and prosperity point of view, this April 2020 had - beside the very bad news of increases in war-related expenses and preparations – the unusually bad COVID-19 pandemic, with extreme protective measures, which just shows again how urgently it is necessary to move to one world system for the world family of over 7.7 B people, as we mentioned many times.

Now some good news: medical robots are in high demand to disinfect surroundings and contain the spread of coronavirus and COVID-19; small, foldable robots will scout regions on the Moon; Amazon said it would spend second-quarter profits (normally around $4 B) on responding to the COVID-19 pandemic; AI is used for drug discovery technology against rare nerve disease; for the first time, a robotic spacecraft caught an old satellite and extended its life.

In this World Monthly Report, which is the 42nd in total, we included the most relevant news, in a balanced approach, usually directly from the source, to help the general public better understand the realities around us. Being well and correctly informed is a sine qua non requirement for everybody, in order to make the right decisions for the future, which future begins to take shape in our recent books. This World Monthly Report provides the information needed for making the best-informed decisions.

Enjoy this World Monthly Report, and be optimist!

Michael M. Dediu, Ph. D.

Nashua, NH, U. S. A., 6 May 2020

Italy, Venezia - In the middle of the west façade of the Basilica di San Marco, we see the central bronze-fashioned door, in a round-arched portal, encircled by polychrome marble columns. Above this door there are three round bas-relief cycles of Romanesque art. A Japanese couple, with their Japanese photographer, make their wedding photographs in this most beautiful place.

Table of Contents

London, from the Shard (2012, 309 m, observatory at 244 m), looking east to the Tower Bridge (1886-1894, combined bascule and suspension turreted bridge over River Thames (flowing from west (left) to east (right)), between London boroughs Tower Hamlets (north – left up) and Southward (south – right), length 244 m, height 65 m, longest span 82 m, clearance 8 m (closed), 42 m (open)), City Hall (2002, height 45 m, center right round, for the Greater London Authority: Mayor of London and the London Assembly).

World Status Report
3 May 2020

There are many more bureaucrats in the world than doctors, but all people want more doctors and no bureaucrats.

Patients need doctors, not bureaucrats.

Health care needs freedom to focus on medical issues.

A Global Innovation Research Institute is needed to work on global medical problems.

The best steps against coronavirus are to use good masks and protective equipment, strong disinfectants, keep at least an arm length distance between people, and continue normal and necessary activities as much as possible, with reasonable limitations when more than 6 people are supposed to be together in a small place (use different shifts, separations, etc.).

At the research level, much more advanced mathematics and AI must be used in the medical research, to find solutions to the COVID-19 problems.

People ask to immediately replace all warfighters on the Planet, with peace-implementors, all warships with peace-ships, all attack enemy plans with join everybody for friendly collaboration plans, and other similar replacements.

While the COVID-19 has many bad consequences, it is important to remember that the difference between the number of world births and the number of world deaths every single day is well over 200,000, therefore the world population is growing really fast.

People say that it is possible to have a good economy, and to find a medical solution for COVID-19 at the same time.

There is much world uncertainty surrounding the magnitude, trajectory, and duration of COVID-19's impact.

Coronavirus will lead to significant economic contraction across the world.

For all the residents of the Planet Earth, scientists, researchers, doctors, first responders, nurses, and police have always been their heroes.

There are no borders in the world for weather, viruses, plants, etc. – people also do not need borders, but just one civilized and friendly country on Earth.

Hyper-regulated health care is not good for people.

There too many intrusive and politically motivated government controls these days.

9 April 2020. Reports: Global COVID-19 cases now number over 1.5 M, with over 430 K reported in the U.S.

All people are very concerned because there is no good world structure, many suffer of malnutrition, white some big farms are dumping milk, beef, etc.

Life on Earth appeared about 4 billions of years ago – now it's time to finally protect all people's life.

Reports: Around the world, rulers are using the pandemic as an excuse to grab more power, and all the people are very concerned.

While coronavirus is a world serious medical problem, it is not at the level of making major policy decisions on fear, rush, chaos and panic alone. There is an unfortunate tendency in the media to exaggerate, and then career politicians everywhere use these exaggerations to implement dangerous policies, which are harmful to liberty and the quality of life. Leaders in the world need to be careful, to listen to doctors and other specialists, and take balanced decisions, not to produce more damages than good results.

All factories in the world should be redeployed to produce healthcare and other necessary supplies for people, not war-related equipment.

Keep calm and carry on your good work for peace, good health, freedom, and prosperity in a better world.

Global security is real only if there are no arms at all.

The probability of war in the world is high (58%), because of the enormous amount of war-related equipment, huge war-related budgets (which use people's money, without their approval), war mentality, war promotion, militarization of space, truth and wisdom are completely missing, misinformation is everywhere, use-related hazards and risks, and the high chances of technical and human errors.

The enemies of the people on Earth are not other people, but viruses, microbes, bad bacteria and hundreds of deadly illnesses – all people on Earth must work together against these real enemies for all of us.

Implementing a global strategy for peace is essential.

World-class leaders must have the talent of leading people to peace, harmony, freedom and prosperity.

All people on Earth are watching what the authorities are doing regarding the Covid-19 (coronavirus).

Status of the world activities for sustainable peace, harmony, freedom, good health, good education, and prosperity: 10% good, 30% neutral, and 60% bad.

World quality of life index: 2.1 (bad) (1 very bad, 10 excellent)

World medical assistance index: 2 (bad) (1 very bad, 10 excellent)

The State of Communications in World Healthcare - Broken

World noise level: unhealthy

World Financial Stability Index: 4 (1 very bad, 10 excellent)

World Food Stability Index: 3 (1 very bad, 10 excellent)

World Freedom Stability Index: 2.1 (1 very bad, 10 excellent)

Electrical Safety Standards Worldwide – good

Business Expectations Index – low

Business Uncertainty Index – high

The arms control regime is disintegrating - the over 7.7 B people on Earth ask for new arms control and complete arms elimination agreements.

- Global security threats increased.
- Global relationships are unstable.

- Preventing emergencies is an expanding area of international cooperation.

- There are international settlement efforts in Libya.

- Genomic surveillance is increasing.

- The mathematical algorithms are becoming more useful every day.

- Some parts of the modern web are becoming unusable and user-hostile wastelands.

- Global monetary policy is not good.

- Global economic outlook is unstable.
- Global inflationary overheating is taking place.
- Global financial imbalances are increasing.

Saving Humanity from war is a major objective for the 7.7 B people on Earth.

The world borderlands are always in danger.

There is a continuous and intense global struggle for peace.

Special attention is needed for global health maintenance and improvement.

The global robotic process automation market is growing fast.

World food instability is a major concern for billions of people.

In the world there is a growing desire by patients to age in place.

Misinformation, disinformation and mal-information are everywhere in the world these days.

The world medical objective is to deliver affordable and high-quality medical care for everybody.

Global standards in many technical areas are strict necessary.

The indefinite extension of the Treaty on Non-Proliferation of Nuclear Weapons (NPT) in 1995 is a good example for having permanent peace-related treaties.

The planet is covered with bacteria and viruses, and we're constantly in contact with them. There must be a world constant medical effort to make sure that all people are protected against the most dangerous bacteria and viruses.

Earth Day is on 22 April 2020.
World Book Day is on 23 April 2020.

The World Ocean is very important for all the people.

The global pandemic is causing a shift in the way world medicine is practiced. Telehealth is gaining more importance, as it has become crucial to ease the strain from healthcare facilities.

According to the World Health Organization in 2016, more than 1.9 billion adults were overweight and 650 millions were obese. People who are overweight or obese are predisposed to developing metabolic diseases, and have an increased risk of mortality. Although diet and physical activity have a direct effect upon weight, genetic factors can also play a role. Therefore, Novo Nordisk is looking to identify gene combinations that may provide protection from obesity and associated metabolic disorders.

Global economists say that oil demand is down 30% worldwide amid travel restrictions and lockdowns.

The general sentiment across the globe is that we are living through difficult times, but the world community is united by this challenge.

Now we have the gravest world crisis the aerospace industry has ever known.

United States of America

(Population 328.2 M, rank 3, growth 0.5%. Free: 89 of 100. Area 9.52 M km^2, rank 4.).

Short Status Report:
- Over $23 T is the U.S. national debt - it is officially greater than the amount of money the U.S. entire economy creates in a year (GDP). And it's only getting worse.
- Financial responsibility is very low.
- Current overall inflation: 5%. It is high, under pressure, and expected to grow to 6 %.
- Credit risk is high.
- Market risk is very high.
- Asset prices are artificially inflated.
- Violent crimes are rising annually
- People should receive 5% interest for their deposits in banks.
- Economic outlook: unfavorable
- There is no Internet in 15% of the U.S. homes – 1 in 7 homes is without Internet.
- In 2019 the real estate taxes increased by over 12.5% compared with one year ago.
- The U.S. student debt is over $1.6 T.
- In 2019 the stocks, artificially inflated with new printed money, were up 8 times more than the wages, 14 times more than the official inflation rate, and 5 times more than the correct inflation rate. More than 45% of Americans do not own stocks.
- The number of unemployed Americans is over 30 M.
- Medical insurance increased in 2020 by over 7.88%.
People pay now 60% more than last year for web hosting services – the inflation is growing fast.
Reports: Trillion-dollar deficits will be with us for years and perhaps decades to come, which is very dangerous.
Pegging the dollar to the gold standard.is a good idea.
There are 44.5 millions of seniors on Social Security.

People in their 50s are laid off. According to researchers, the situation is common, and older workers have a harder time finding a new job.

Because of the production and sales of arms, mass shootings continue, and thousands of people are killed and wounded each year.

On 30 March 2020, the governor of Virginia issued a stay-at-home order that requires individuals to remain in their residences, and extends the directive to maintain social distancing, and prohibit gatherings of more than 10 people until, therefore many companies and organizations will remain closed through 10 June 2020.

Reports: An economically bloated $2.2 T spending relief bill, an amount greater than the GDP of the majority of the countries It is only the third massive relief bill, and we've been told several trillions of dollars more would have to get spent. Then there are the trillions of dollars more of Federal Reserve Board liquidity injections – the people are very concerned. The politicians believe that sending $1,200 checks to people will "stimulate" the economy. Among the many mistaken provisions of this new law is a welfare benefit to workers, that pays them more money if they quit and become unemployed, than if they stay on the job – very bad for all people.

Reports: In our present coronavirus crises, the Senate Minority Leader pleaded for the President to use the Stafford Act to release disaster relief money. The President not only invoked the Stafford Act, but also the National Emergency Act, and "the Korean War-era Defense Production Act, which enables presidents to direct industrial production toward war needs, when national security or natural disaster requires it." Certainly, the people are very concerned seeing that the President would immediately seek to use all the powers that have been given by previous Congresses. Last Friday, 27 march, when negotiations with General Motors on making ventilators did not move fast enough, the President utilized the Defense Production Act to force General Motors to make the ventilators. The U.S. Constitution, designed to have separate and distinct powers between Congress and the executive branch, has eroded over many administrations and congresses. Very dangerously, each crisis has given more power to the executive branch.

Reports: While all too many who make policy can theoretically do their jobs from anywhere, for many of the more common, service style workers, work is a destination. It involves meeting the needs of people in person. When politicians at all levels imposed a lockdown on the U.S. economy, they rather unkindly wrecked the earnings capabilities of all too many persons.

Reports: This coronavirus crisis shows us that we have internal problems posed by our own government and its bureaucracy. The Centers for Disease Control and Prevention and Food and Drug Administration are two prime examples. We would like, for example, to be able to scale up society's coronavirus testing abilities. However, the FDA has banned anyone from offering home testing kits, a massive bureaucratic barrier to the nation's capabilities in this time of crisis. This is not the only such problem. The two government agencies have delayed the development and roll out of hospital-based coronavirus tests as well. In the middle of a global crisis, the government screwed up — and then waited five weeks to fix it.

Reports: The "stimulus" package just passed by the Senate has nothing to do with "supply side", or the reduction of barriers to production. Quite the opposite. The federal government has money to spend, or the capacity to borrow in order to spend, because the American people are productive, and the federal government has sadly arrogated to itself enormous amounts of that production. The federal government only has $2 T to hand out based on economic growth that's already happened. The bad "stimulus" package will reduce the economic growth.

31 March 2020. Reports: Moody's Investors Service has lowered its outlook on U.S. corporate debt from stable to negative, saying that a coronavirus recession will result in rising default rates. The situation is especially troubling as non-financial corporate debt totaled $6.6 T at the end of 2019, a 78% increase since the last Great Recession ended in mid-2009.

Reports: There are many more victims of gun violence than of coronavirus, and the people are very concerned.

U.S. crude oil experienced its worst month and quarter in history.

Rep. Andy Biggs (R-AZ) mentioned recently that it is time America went back to work. People want to work. We understand that self-sufficiency and meaningful employment are part of the good life. Some medical leaders have advised us to distance ourselves from each other and to lock ourselves into our homes. The vast majority of the country has undertaken these measures, and heeded the counsel regarding improving our hygienic habits. Our caregivers and first responders have undertaken risks to themselves to provide assistance to our communities. We all are grateful to them. I advocate that we continue to follow the patterns of behavior that will reduce the risk of community spread. At some point, though, we cross from a mitigation period of separation, to inducing health and societal problems from poverty and economic duress.

7 April 2020. Rep. Andy Biggs (R-Ariz.) also mentioned that even before the CARES Act was signed into law, the national debt stood at $23.6 T. Now we will add at least $2 T to this already unsustainable sum. The tragedy unfolding, in addition to the horrid takeaway of our liberties and right to work, is that while more and more Americans can work from anywhere, tens of millions cannot, as evidenced by the layoffs.

8 April 2020. Reports: In a recent survey of 10,000 Americans fielded in the midst of the coronavirus crisis, respondents said "My Employer" was better prepared to manage this crisis than "My Country" by a stunning 15%, 45% to 30%. Communications coming from "My Employer" were more trusted (63%) than from Government (58%) or Media (51%).

Rep. Andy Biggs (R-AZ) recently mentioned that Americans must decide if government is by the people, or by elected executives with a penchant for abusing our rights, regardless of whether they are in the federal government, states, and local jurisdictions. Can we trust Americans to operate in our society by reasonable recommendations to keep the public safe, and reduce the risk of transmission of disease, or have we decided that we simply cannot accept the risks of freedom any longer? Some people are now showing their authoritarian bent. It isn't just that we are emasculating our economy and running the risk of triggering an economic depression; it is that we are undermining the very essence of America. If we don't reopen our businesses and economy, and we allow the constriction of our rights—if we allow the government at every level to accrete more power over every aspect of our lives—will we be America any longer?

Senator Rand Paul (R-KY) has also partnered with fellow Sen. Joni Ernst of Iowa on legislation to abolish the Presidential Election Campaign Fund, which has seen a massive decrease in popularity among taxpayers, and use its over $360 M balance to provide even more tests, masks and other personal protective equipment.

Reports: After the coronavirus crisis struck, in America there was bipartisan support in Congress to spend trillions of dollars. Which of course adds greatly to concern about what the national debt will have on our future. Wrongfully, Congress could care less about my grandchildren's future. Republicans and Democrats are totally focused on this year's elections for president, Senate and House of Representatives, and they are buying votes by giving money to their favorite special interest groups. Both parties are openly buying votes. It was decided the virus crisis was a good time to give $35 M to the Kennedy Center, which got whittled down to only $25 M. A few days after appropriating the money, the Center laid off the National Symphony Orchestra. A gift to the Kennedy Center needs tradeoffs to other Member of Congress. Thus a $150 M in grants was authorized to the National Endowment of the Arts and National Endowment of the Humanities.

Reports: Six of the 10 counties with the largest population gains this decade were in Texas — Harris, Tarrant, Bexar, Dallas, Collin, and Travis — according to the U.S. Census Bureau's July 1, 2019, population estimates. In the U. S. there are 384 metropolitan statistical areas, 542 micropolitan statistical areas, and 3,142 counties.

Community Colleges Month: April 2020

National Library Week: April 19-25, 2020
National Kindergarten Day: April 21, 2020
National Arbor Day: April 24, 2020
National Telephone Day: April 25, 2020

For 2020, U.S. academic researchers will have at their disposal about $90.1 billions-worth of research funds, or about 14.8% of the total U.S. R&D expenditure ($609 B). Individual U.S. academic institutions will invest about $23.2 billions (or about 3.8% of the total U.S. R&D investment) of their own resources to support this R&D.

15 April 2020. Reports: It was decided to shut down the House of Representatives for a month.

U.S. retail sales plunged 8.7% in March, while manufacturing output slumped by the most in over 74 years.

The first time since WWII, the nation will owe more than its economy can produce in a given year.

People are concerned about the loss to the central bank's independence.

Reports: The U. S. are facing the worst economic disaster since the Great Depression. In less than a month, over 22 M Americans have lost their jobs. People can't let this crisis go on so long that it creates an opportunity for uncontrolled politicians to trample on people's liberties.

Several Southern leaders across Georgia, South Carolina and Tennessee moved to reopen their local economies.

Reports: The state of Missouri has sued the Chinese government, and other top Chinese institutions, for the role they played in handling the COVID-19 pandemic.

24 April 2020. Reports: 16 states unveiled plans to lift coronavirus restrictions. Data yesterday, 23 April, showed 4.4 M

Americans filed for unemployment benefits last week, bringing the 5-week total to more than 26 M, and wiping out all job gains since the previous global financial crisis, 12 years ago.

Reports: As of April 26th, 43 states, along with 4 U.S. Territories, and the District of Columbia, "have ordered or recommended school building closures for the rest of the academic year, affecting approximately 45.1 millions of public school students." These sudden and mass closures have forced schools to lower standards on everything.

Reports: Rep. Andy Biggs (R-AZ) & Rep. Ken Buck (R-CO) mentioned recently that the federal government had a wrong response to a coronavirus crisis of its own making. It is amazing how intensely foolish the political class was, regardless of Party. To fight a health scare with forced economic desperation brings new meaning to obtuse, but then politicians, aided by others, have been wrecking precious lives for millennia. This is what they do.

Reports: Federal bailouts for states under the auspices of coronavirus relief legislation are "covering up for the killing of our economy that's been done by the governors," said Rep. Thomas Massie (R-KY). Massie warned of moral hazard associated with the federal transfer of monies to states operating under various types of economic restrictions such as shelter-in-place and stay-at-home orders. "By sending money into the states, and into the companies, and into the hands of everybody, we are basically covering up for the killing of the economy that's been done by the governors," cautioned Massie. These governors should open their economies back up, but if we keep paying for the shutdown, the governors are going to keep it shut down.

Reports: Looking to keep the money flowing, and totally ignoring the deficit, the central bank is buying up to $500 B worth of state and local government bonds. Purchases of the paper will be in effect for counties with at least 500 K residents, and cities with at least 250 K residents (the previous cutoffs were 2 M and 1 M, respectively). This will allow for up to 261 state, city, and county issuers, up from just 76 previously, with the longest maturity extended to up to three years, from two years previously.

Reports: Rep. Tom McClintock (R-CA) mentioned that the accumulating death toll from COVID-19 can be seen minute-by-minute, but there's another death toll few seem to care much about: the number of poverty-related deaths being set in motion by deliberately plunging millions of Americans into poverty and despair.

Reports: The governmental response to a virus that amounted to fighting something potentially lethal, with economic contraction, is not adequate, because the economic contraction is primarily endured by those with the least.

Reports: On April 9, 2020, the United States reported an outbreak of a Highly Pathogenic Avian Influenza (HPAI) in the state of South Carolina.

Reports: COVID-19 caused 3 new hires for every 10 layoffs.

Reports: Death rates always go up due to prolonged economic hardship.

Reports: About 20% of Americans were already living with mental health challenges before COVID-19.

Reports: Because of Covid-19, some parents are postponing well-child checkups, including shots, putting millions of children at risk of exposure to preventable deadly diseases.

Reports: Serious problems will appear down the road, given the borrowing spree that both the U.S. government and Corporate America have been on since 1 March.

Reports: Rep. Ken Buck (R-CO) mentioned that officials have shut down our economy, added trillions to our nation's debt, and put more than 26 millions of people out of work. To make matters worse, elected officials are tossing the Constitution aside, going so far as criminalizing the sale of gardening equipment, and arresting parents for tossing a ball with their children in deserted public parks. The Constitution is not something that can be tossed out at the whim of a public servant. It is a set of rights available to every American and should be safeguarded by those elected to serve.

Reports: These draconian policy decisions will have lasting impacts on our nation and incomplete and unreliable data are driving our nation's response to the coronavirus. The models we rely on for realistic predictions have shown to be inaccurate and are being revised downward frequently.

3 May 2020. Reports: The coronavirus pandemic, now going into its eighth week, has exposed so many flaws in our nation's healthcare system. We have shortages of doctors and nurses, because of restrictive licensing requirements. We have a shortage of equipment, because of trade barriers stemming the flow of materials from abroad. We also have a shortage of money, because of our government's reckless spending on other nonsense over the years. One thing we're also running short on is time. More than 30 millions of people have now filed for unemployment

Reports: Just a few closures of meat packing plants are putting the entire meat industry on the brink of collapse. There are restrictions on over 1,000 small meat processing plants that aren't allowed to supply restaurants, schools, hotels, and the like. The American people are dependent on a few big businesses that enjoy great advantages thanks to regulation.

3 May 2020. Reports: Just one day after announcing that the House would return to Washington on May 4th, Democrats reversed course, and delayed their return to an unknown date.

Puerto Rico: (Population 3.6 M, rank 134, decrease 0.1%; an unincorporated territory of the United States, located in the northeast Caribbean Sea, 1,600 km southeast of Miami, Florida.).

United Nations. (UN) There are 195 officially recognized countries. Around 44,000 people work for the United Nations. There is a wide range of jobs: Researchers, IT-specialists, lawyers, experts on finance and administration, or translators work at the New York headquarters, at the official locations, or at specialized agencies. More than half of the UN's workforce is employed in the field, in projects of humanitarian aid, or on peace missions.

G20 group members are European Union (EU) and 19 countries: Argentina, Australia, Brazil, Canada, China, France, Germany, India, Indonesia, Italy, Japan, Mexico, Republic of Korea, Republic of South Africa, Russia, Saudi Arabia, Turkey, United Kingdom, United States of America.

The Group of Seven (G7) is a group consisting of Canada, France, Germany, Italy, Japan, the United Kingdom, and the United States. The G8 format (the G7 and Russia) had been in place for 16 years, from 1998-2014.

Netherlands, 14 Aug 1977, Amsterdam (1275, population 1.3 M, elevation minus 2 m (2 m under the Atlantic Ocean level)): Zijkanaal G, with a bridge for the street s150, and Havenstraat on the left.

China, Japan, and neighbors

China: (Population 1.4 B, rank 1, growth 0.4%. Freedom House reports for 2019: Not Free (10 of 100). Area 9.59 M km^2, rank 3).

18 April 2020. Xinhua: Xi Jinping, general secretary of the Communist Party of China (CPC) Central Committee, on Friday, 17 April, chaired a leadership meeting on regular COVID-19 epidemic prevention and control measures. The meeting of the Political Bureau of the CPC Central Committee also studied the current economic situation and made arrangements for economic work.

The meeting came two days after Xi presided over a meeting of the Standing Committee of the Political Bureau of the CPC Central Committee, also on the epidemic response and economic situation.

Friday's meeting pointed out that while the positive momentum in China's epidemic response is being consolidated, the task remains formidable, requiring control measures on a regular basis, and strengthened efforts to guard against both imported infections and domestic rebounds. The meeting stressed continuous epidemic response measures in hard-hit Hubei Province and its capital city of Wuhan, including extensive nucleic acid testing among key population groups and those who volunteer to get tested.

The epidemic prevention and control work in Beijing should be further strengthened, while targeted measures should be taken across the country to guard against rebounds in cases, according to the meeting.

The meeting also called for building a stronger defense at border cities against the virus, stressing better allocating medical resources and improving quarantine and testing capacities in these cities.

"The first quarter of 2020 was extremely unusual," a statement issued after the meeting said, noting that the sudden COVID-19 outbreak had an unprecedented impact on China's economic and social development. China's economy has demonstrated great resilience, the statement said, adding that work and production are gradually getting back to normal levels, with the rapid development of many new industries and businesses amid the epidemic.

The meeting underlined upholding the underlying principle of pursuing progress while ensuring stability. Efforts must be made to ensure that the epidemic will not rebound, while steadying the economic fundamentals and securing people's basic livelihood.

In this regard, the country will have to take the initiative to advance work resumption at all fronts with regular COVID-19 epidemic prevention and control measures in place, and fight the epidemic persistently in a bid to bring the economic and social activities completely back to normal, according to the meeting.

The meeting noted that China will use stronger macro policy tools to cushion the epidemic fallout.

It called for more proactive fiscal measures such as issuing special government bonds to support the virus fight, and increasing the issuance of local government bonds as well as raising the utilization efficiency of capital to help stabilize the economy.

Monetary policies should be more flexible and balanced and instruments such as reserve requirement ratio cuts, interest rate reductions and re-loans should be fully leveraged to ensure reasonable and sufficient liquidity, and a lower interest rate in the loan market, the meeting said, stressing the need to channel capital into the real economy, especially medium-sized, small and micro enterprises. In emphasizing the need to expand domestic demand, the meeting said it is necessary to release the potential of consumption by stimulating consumer spending and increasing public spending as appropriate. It's also imperative to expand investment by way of renovating old and dilapidated residential areas, strengthening investment in traditional and new infrastructure to advance upgrading of traditional industries, and boosting investment in emerging strategic industries.

Support should be given to sales of export products in the domestic market. Measures will be taken to improve small and medium-sized firms' abilities to survive and thrive, including advancing tax and fee cuts, and lowering financing and rental costs of the firms.

China will also make efforts to maintain the stability and competitiveness of the country's industrial and supply chains, and ensure the full completion of the poverty eradication target on schedule, said the meeting. The meeting stressed efforts to push forward reform and firmly promote wider opening-up. The country will facilitate the smooth flow of international logistics, strictly control the quality of epidemic prevention and control supplies for export, and jointly advance high-quality development under the Belt and Road Initiative.

22 April 2020. Xinhua: Xi Jinping, general secretary of the Communist Party of China Central Committee, on Tuesday, 21 April, stressed the importance of employment in follow-up measures to help people shake off poverty, during an inspection tour in northwest China's Shaanxi Province.

Xi made the remarks while visiting a community in Laoxian Town, Pingli County of the city of Ankang.

The community is now home to 1,346 households that have been relocated from hilly, geological disaster-prone, or poverty-stricken areas across the town. At the home of resident Wang Xianping, Xi sat and had a chat with Wang's family about their daily life.

Relocated people can only live in peace and contentment when they have a stable life, which depends on employment, Xi said.

He stressed down-to-earth efforts facilitating employment, warning against any practice of formalities for formalities' sake.

The places Xi visited in this inspection tour are located in the Qinling-Bashan mountainous region, one of China's 14 contiguous areas of extreme poverty, which are the "hardest nut to crack" in the final rush period for poverty relief.

Across China, more than 9.6 millions of poor people have been relocated to more inhabitable areas over the past couple of years as part of the country's poverty alleviation efforts.

Addressing a symposium in March on securing a decisive victory in poverty alleviation, Xi stressed that lifting all rural residents living below the current poverty line, out of poverty by 2020, is a solemn commitment made by the CPC Central Committee, and it must be fulfilled on schedule.

25 April 2020. Xinhua: At a time when the world economy is plagued by the coronavirus pandemic, policymakers across the globe are faced with the same dilemma: how to get the economy back on track amid containment of the virus?

With new cases dwindling, China is among the very first countries that are able to explore ways of restarting its economic engine while keeping the virus under control.

The trajectory of the Chinese economy toward more steady growth in the long run has not changed, said Chinese President Xi Jinping during an inspection tour from Monday, 20 April, to Thursday, 23 April, in northwest China's Shaanxi Province, urging more efforts to accelerate the transformation of economic growth modes and firm up the real economy, especially the manufacturing sector.

Since COVID-19 has been basically contained domestically, Xi, also general secretary of the Communist Party of China (CPC) Central Committee and chairman of the Central Military Commission, has personally chaired a number of key meetings themed on coordinating epidemic control and business resumption, offering the world insights into when to restart an economy and how.

Virus-control as precondition. After over two months of lockdown, Wuhan, the Chinese city hardest hit by the novel coronavirus outbreak, lifted its outbound travel restrictions on April 8.

The decision to lift the lockdown, just like the one imposing it, required both cautious assessment and courage in policymaking.

Hubei Province first reported zero increase in confirmed cases on March 18, a milestone for the main battlefield of the anti-virus fight. Previously, new confirmed cases elsewhere in the country had been declining for more than a month. "The economy is a dynamic circulating system that cannot afford a long-term disruption," Xi said during an important speech in Beijing in February.

But lifting certain restrictions does not mean the country has eased its epidemic control efforts. Across the country, strict quarantine measures were taken to ensure the hard-won results be maintained.

While the positive momentum in China's epidemic prevention and control is being consolidated, the task remains formidable, requiring control measures on a regular basis and strengthened efforts to guard against both imported infections and domestic rebounds, according to a recent meeting of the Political Bureau of the CPC Central Committee chaired by Xi.

During his inspection in March to a port in Ningbo of eastern China's Zhejiang Province, Xi said that things could gradually get back to normal amid a positive trend in epidemic control, but also cautioned against a potential comeback of the virus.

"Although the vast majority of regions in the country are now at low risk, it is not yet time to think everything is fine. We need to be careful and patient," he said.

The country is restarting its economy in a gradual and orderly manner. Factories and grocery stores were among the first to resume operation, followed by restaurants and barbershops. Depending on the risks of different regions, schools are scheduled to reopen, while indoor sports venues will soon receive customers.

"With continued epidemic prevention and control as a precondition, we must now actively push forward the resumption of work and production, ensuring not only production tasks but also people's health," Xi said during his inspection in Zhejiang.

Region-specific measures.

In coordinating epidemic control and business resumption, China has avoided a "one-size-fits-all" approach and resorted to more targeted measures to revive different regions.

"Region-specific, multi-level targeted approaches to business resumption must be implemented," Xi said in the February speech.

According to a national guideline, regions with relatively low risk should focus on preventing imported cases and comprehensively restoring the order of production and life. Medium-risk regions should promote work and production resumption in an orderly manner, while high-risk regions should continue to be fully committed to epidemic prevention and control.

Local authorities have been on high alert to adjust epidemic response measures according to dynamic changes in risk levels. Wuhan has shifted its focus to business resumption as the city is now categorized into a low-risk region. Chaoyang District of Beijing, on the other hand, was categorized into a high-risk region for clustered infections reported in the past week and is required to take stringent virus control measures. The Chinese health authority has also scaled up testing and treatment for COVID-19 infections in border areas, as the country faces a rising risk of imported cases.

Precise support. Xi has paid special attention to those vulnerable groups impacted by COVID-19. The country's small and medium-sized enterprises (SMEs), contributing an increasing share to the economy, were among the hardest hit by the virus as strict quarantine measures dampened demand and strained cash flows.

Right after the basic containment of the virus, Xi paid a visit to Zhejiang Province, where SMEs account for a major part of the local economy. Stressing that the CPC Central Committee has kept SMEs and private firms in mind when making policies, Xi said that more targeted measures will be introduced to help them tide over difficulties. "We will prevent the SMEs from being fundamentally weakened, help them recover to a good state, and have new development as soon as possible," Xi said.

Large state-owned enterprises should lead enterprises in both upstream and downstream sectors, as well as SMEs, to fully resume production and work with regular epidemic control measures in place, Xi said Wednesday, 22 April, while inspecting work resumption and economic recovery in Xi'an, the provincial capital of Shaanxi.

Rather than initiating a "flood-like" stimulus to shore up the economy, the country has resorted to targeted cuts in reserve requirement ratios for small banks, to channel funds into SMEs, and stepped up fiscal support, reducing taxes and fees for these firms.

As of mid-April, about 84% of SMEs have resumed businesses, data from the Ministry of Industry and Information Technology showed. Special care was also given to low-income groups, who are faced with mounting pressure as COVID-19 deprived many jobs and posed new challenges to the country's poverty relief work.

During his inspection tour to Shaanxi, Xi sat down with local residents, who were relocated from poverty-stricken areas, and stressed the importance of securing employment for relocated people, to settle down in their new homes, make more money, and not fall back into poverty.

"Being lifted out of poverty is not an end in itself, but the starting point of a new life and a new pursuit," he said. Like the remarks he made while inspecting Zhejiang Province, Xi once again stressed the importance of turning crises into opportunities.

"We must stay good at seizing and creating opportunities from the current crises and challenges and continue to develop new models, forms of business, technologies and products, so as to create new and greater achievements and reach new heights," he said.

28 April 2020. Xinhua: Xi Jinping, general secretary of the Communist Party of China (CPC) Central Committee, on Monday, 27 April, presided over the 13th meeting of the Central Commission for Comprehensively Deepening Reform.

Xi, also Chinese president, chairman of the Central Military Commission, and head of the Central Commission for Comprehensively Deepening Reform, stressed efforts to deepen reform, improve institutions, improve the governance system, and make good use of institutional strengths to respond to risks and challenges. The fundamental reason behind China's solid progress in epidemic prevention and control, as well as work and production resumption, lies in the advantages of the CPC leadership and the socialist system, he said. The meeting deliberated and passed a plan on securing public health emergency supplies, a guideline on reforming the system for regulating medical insurance funds, a plan on reforming the ChiNext market, a plan on protecting and restoring major national ecosystems, a guideline for boosting the healthy growth of young people, and the implementation plan of major reform measures taken at the fourth plenary session of the 19th CPC Central Committee. Medical insurance funds must be well managed and used, said a statement released after the meeting.

To fight COVID-19, China has rolled out timely policies to include COVID-19 diagnosis and treatment in the scope of payments by medical insurance funds, demonstrating the strengths of the Chinese socialist system, the statement said. The meeting stressed efforts to safeguard social fairness and justice and promote the healthy and sustainable development of the medical security system.

Promoting the reform of the ChiNext board, and piloting the registration-based initial public offering system, are crucial arrangements for deepening capital market reforms, optimizing the capital market's basic system, and improving capital market functions, the statement said.

It also stressed ecological protection and restoration, calling for scientific layout of major projects for the protection and restoration of important ecosystems across the country. Reform should be pushed to better coordinate the study and the physical exercise of juveniles for their healthy growth, the statement said.

The meeting stressed reforms of institutional mechanisms to boost scientific and technological innovation capacity, as well as the capacity to cope with emergencies. Meanwhile, reform measures conducive to promoting work resumption, employment, investment and consumption, as well as the development of smaller firms should be reinforced, the statement said.

Monday's meeting was attended by Li Keqiang, Wang Huning and Han Zheng, who are members of the Standing Committee of the Political Bureau of the CPC Central Committee and deputy heads of the Central Commission for Comprehensively Deepening Reform.

30 April 2020. Xinhua: Xi Jinping, general secretary of the Communist Party of China (CPC) Central Committee, on Wednesday chaired a leadership meeting on regular epidemic prevention and control and supporting the economic and social development in Hubei Province.The meeting of the Standing Committee of the Political Bureau of the CPC Central Committee analyzed the COVID-19 situation at home and abroad.

Xi said arduous efforts have brought a decisive outcome to the fight of defending Hubei and its capital city Wuhan, and the nationwide battle against the epidemic has gained major strategic achievements. The COVID-19 pandemic continues its explosive growth overseas, Xi said, noting the mounting pressure to prevent imported infections and the growing complexity of stemming domestic epidemic resurgence. He demanded no relaxation in epidemic control to safeguard the hard-earned achievements.

All regions and departments should implement in detail the regular epidemic control measures to provide a solid guarantee to the full recovery of economic and social order, Xi said. Stressing epidemic prevention and control in key areas and groups, Xi asked Heilongjiang Province in northeast China to make particular efforts to prevent infections in hospitals and go all-out to treat patients.

Hubei, including Wuhan, should continue strengthening community-level epidemic prevention and control, Xi said, also urging Beijing to continue implementing key prevention and control tasks. Xi also emphasized epidemic control at transportation facilities and tourist sites during the upcoming five-day May Day holiday and asked schools to reopen in an orderly manner.

The meeting demanded improving the accuracy and effectiveness of measures taken to prevent imported COVID-19 cases.

China will continue to help relevant countries to the best of its ability, step up quality supervision of anti-epidemic supplies and continue to make active contributions to international cooperation on fighting COVID-19.

The meeting noted that people in Hubei, especially those in Wuhan, have made great contributions to and great sacrifices for epidemic control, and the province is facing difficulties in promoting economic and social development and ensuring people's livelihood. The CPC Central Committee has discussed and endorsed a package of policies for supporting the economic and social development in

Hubei, specifying measures in fiscal, taxation, financial, credit, investment and foreign trade aspects.

Party committees and governments at all levels in Hubei were asked to accelerate the return to normal work and life order on the precondition of regular epidemic control.

Residents' employment and basic needs should be guaranteed while policies supporting people most in need should be implemented, the meeting noted, adding that all poor population must be lifted out of poverty. The meeting also emphasized the need to accelerate work resumption and business reopening, help companies especially micro, small and medium-sized enterprises address difficulties, and promote the recovery of pillar industries such as auto manufacturing, electronic information, new materials and bio-medicine.

A number of important projects must be launched, and the construction of traditional and new infrastructures such as 5G and artificial intelligence must be sped up, the meeting said.

It stressed accelerating farm production and expanding sales channels for agricultural products to boost income for farmers.

It also emphasized enhancing public health and other emergency response systems to better address major emergencies.

3 May 2020. Xinhua: Chinese President Xi Jinping has encouraged the young Chinese to hold firm convictions, and develop genuine skills, to devote themselves to the great cause of building a great country. Xi, also general secretary of the Communist Party of China Central Committee and chairman of the Central Military Commission, made the statement on Sunday, 3 May, when sending greetings to the young people across the country ahead of China's Youth Day, which falls on May 4.

Hong Kong. (Population 7.3 M, rank 104, growth 0.8%. Partly Free: 61 of 100).

Macau (Population 622 K, rank 167, growth 1.7 %.)

Taiwan: (Population 23.6 M, rank 56, growth 0.3%. Free, 91 of 100).

Japan (Population 127.5 M, rank 11, decrease 0.2%. Free, 96 of 100).

Afghanistan: (Population 35.5 M, rank 40, growth 2.5%. Not free: 24 of 100).

South Korea: (Population 50.9 M, rank 27, growth 0.4%. Free, 82 of 100).

North Korea: (Population 25.4 M, rank 52, growth 0.5%. Not free: 3 of 100).
19 April 2020. Reports: North Korea continued its show of force this week, launching multiple short-range anti-ship cruise missiles into the sea, and firing air-to-surface missiles from its Sukhoi jets.
3 May 2020. Reports: Some shooting took place close to the border of North Korea with South Korea.

Vietnam (Population 95.5 M, rank 15, growth 1%. Not free, 20 of 100, Socialist Republic of Vietnam).

Laos (Population. 6.8 M, rank 106, growth 1.5%. Not free: 12 of 100).

Cambodia (Population 16 M, rank 71, growth 1.5%. Not Free 31 of 100).

Mongolia (Population 3 M, rank 137, growth 1.6%. Free 85 of 100)

Nepal: (Population 29.3 M, rank 48, growth 1.1%. Partly free 52 of 100).

Russia, Switzerland, Eastern Europe

Russia: (Population 146 M, rank 9, growth 0%. Not free: 20 of 100. Area 17 M km^2, rank 1)

10 April 2020. Vladimir Putin had a telephone conversation with President of the United States of America, Donald Trump, and King of Saudi Arabia, Salman bin Abdulaziz Al Saud.

The discussion focused on the oil market situation, including in view of the talks at the OPEC+ extraordinary ministerial meeting, and the forthcoming videoconference of the G20 energy ministers.

The parties confirmed their commitment to coordinate actions on stabilizing the situation in global oil trade, and minimizing the negative effect of oil price volatility on the global economy.

10 April 2020. Vladimir Putin had a telephone conversation with US President Donald Trump, at the initiative of the American side. The presidents exchanged views on the current developments in the global oil market, including the tentative OPEC+ agreement on reducing production volumes in order to stabilize oil prices. Donald Trump shared information about his contacts with the leaders of several oil-producing countries. The presidents agreed to continue Russian-American consultations on the issue.

Vladimir Putin and Donald Trump also discussed the coronavirus pandemic, and gave an assessment to the actions being taken in Russia and the United States to prevent the spread of the virus.

Some topical aspects of bilateral relations were covered, including cooperation in space.

As of 13 April 2020, there were 18,328 confirmed cases in Russia. 148 people have passed away, and 2,558 have recovered.

17 April 2020. Vladimir Putin had a telephone conversation with President of the People's Republic of China, Xi Jinping.

It was stressed during an in-depth discussion of the developments in the coronavirus pandemic that mutual support in countering this global threat is further evidence of the special nature of the Russian-Chinese comprehensive strategic partnership. The two leaders reaffirmed their commitment to further strengthening their cooperation in this area, including the exchange of experts and medical equipment, medicines and protective gear.

Vladimir Putin praised the consistent and effective actions of Russia's Chinese partners, which helped stabilize the epidemiological situation in the country. He stressed that it was counterproductive to accuse China of releasing information to the global community on this dangerous infection in an untimely manner. The two leaders expressed confidence that the countries would be able to successfully overcome pandemic-related challenges if they continue to cooperate closely with each other.

The positive development of bilateral relations in general, including the continuous growth of mutual trade, was noted.

The leaders also touched upon current international issues. They agreed that Russia and China would further coordinate their diplomatic efforts.

25 April 2020. In a joint statement by President of the Russian Federation Vladimir Putin and President of the United States of America Donald Trump, commemorating the 75th Anniversary of the meeting on the Elbe, it is mentioned that April 25, 2020, marks the 75th Anniversary of the historic meeting between Soviet and American soldiers, who shook hands on the damaged bridge over the Elbe River, in Germany.

25 April 2020. Russian Prime Minister Mikhail Mishustin mentioned that he has just found out that he tested positive for the coronavirus. As such, he must self-isolate and follow doctors' orders. He suggested appointing Andrei Belousov as Acting Prime Minister, and the Russian President approved.

Switzerland: (Population 8.4 M, rank 99, growth 0.9%. Free: 96 of 100).

Austria: (Population 8.7 M, rank 98, growth 0.3%. Free: 95 of 100).

Poland: (Population 38.1 M, rank 37, decrease 0.1%. Free: 89 of 100).

Croatia: (Population 4.1 M, rank 129, decrease 0.6%. Free: 87 of 100).

Finland: (Population 5.5 M, rank 116, growth 0.4%. Free: 100 of 100).

Romania (Population: 19.6 M, rank 59, decrease 0.5%. Free: 84 of 100)

Moldova: (Population: 4 M, rank 132, decrease 0.2%. Partly Free: 62 of 100).

Belarus: (Population: 9.4 M, rank 93, decrease 0.1%. Not Free: 20 of 100).

Bulgaria: (Population: 7 M, rank 105, decrease 0.7%. Free: 80 of 100).
Reports: In marketing year (MY) 2019/20, Bulgaria's total grain harvest was 8.5% above MY 2018/19, including almost 4 millions of metric tons (MMT) of corn, a production record. Higher domestic stocks, favorable export demand, and lower domestic consumption, supported the increase in exports.

Slovenia: (Population: 2 M, rank 148, growth 0.1%. Free: 92 of 100).

Slovakia: (Population: 5.4 M, rank 117, growth 0.1%. Free: 89 of 100).

Hungary: (Population: 9.7 M, rank 91, decrease 0.3%. Free: 76 of 100)

Ukraine: (Population: 44.2 M, rank 32, decrease 0.5%. Partly free: 61 of 100).

Latvia: (Population: 1.9 M, rank 150, decrease 1.1%. Free: 87 of 100).

Lithuania: (Population: 2.8 M, rank 141, decrease 0.6%. Free: 91 of 100).

Estonia: (Population: 1.3 M, rank 155, decrease 0.2%. Free: 94 of 100).

Serbia: (including Kosovo: Population: 8.7 M, rank 97, decrease 0.3%. Free: 76 of 100.

2 April 2020. Vladimir Putin had a telephone conversation with President of Serbia, Aleksandar Vucic, at the Serbian side's initiative. The presidents discussed the measures taken by the two countries to counter the coronavirus pandemic, as well as opportunities for practical cooperation in this area.

The two leaders agreed on the provision of humanitarian aid to Serbia in order to fight the spread of the infection, in the spirit of traditional friendly bilateral relations. This aid, including sending experts, will mostly be provided by the Russian Defense Ministry.

Reports: On 15 March, Serbia imposed a state of emergency that includes a police curfew, due to the spread of the COVID-19 virus. This will likely delay spring planting due to limitations on the movement of farmers, the lack of seasonal workers, and difficulties in obtaining planting material.

Kosovo ((Disputed: recognized by 110 countries, and not recognized by Serbia, Russia, and others) Population: 1.8 M, Partly free: 52 of 100).

Bosnia and Herzegovina: (Population: 3.5 M, rank 135, decrease 0.3%. Partly free: 55 of 100).

Turkey: (Population 80.7 M, rank 19, growth 1.2%. Partly free: 38 of 100).

2 April 2020. Vladimir Putin had a telephone conversation with President of the Republic of Turkey, Recep Tayyip Erdogan, at the Turkish side's initiative.

The presidents discussed developments related to the spread of the coronavirus pandemic, and exchanged information on measures taken to combat this infection. Particular attention was paid to cooperation in repatriating Russian citizens who are in Turkey.

They continued a substantive exchange of views on the Syrian settlement, including the implementation of the Russian-Turkish agreements of March 5, 2020, to stabilize the situation in the Idlib zone. The Libyan agenda was also discussed. In addition, the leaders spoke about a number of current issues on the bilateral agenda, with a focus on trade and economic cooperation.

The presidents agreed to continue communication at various levels.

21 April 2020. Vladimir Putin had a telephone conversation with President of the Republic of Turkey, Recep Tayyip Erdogan.

The discussion focused on a range of issues related to the spread of the coronavirus. The presidents expressed their preparedness to build up joint efforts in the fight against the infection, including through the health ministries and other relevant agencies, and to continue close coordination to ensure the return of Russian and Turkish citizens to their homelands.

The presidents of Russia and Turkey had a detailed exchange of views on developments in Syria, including the implementation of agreements on the Idlib de-escalation zone, primarily the Additional Protocol to the Sochi Memorandum of September 17, 2018, adopted in Moscow on March 5, 2020. The need for unconditional compliance with the principles of sovereignty and territorial integrity of the Syrian Arab Republic was reaffirmed. At the same time, the presidents emphasized the importance of further close cooperation between Russia and Turkey through military and diplomatic channels.

In addition, current issues of Russian-Turkish cooperation were addressed, primarily in the trade and economic sphere, including the implementation of joint projects in the nuclear energy sector, and the expansion of cooperation in the agriculture and transport.

The presidents agreed on further maintaining regular contact at various levels.

Greece: (Population 11.1 M, rank 82, decrease 0.2%. Free: 84 of 100).

Republic of North Macedonia: (Population 2 M, rank 147, growth 0.1%. Partly Free: 57 of 100).

Albania: (Population 2.9 M, rank 139, growth 0.1%. Partly free: 68 of 100).

Cyprus: (Population 1.1 M, rank 159, growth 0.8%. Free: 94 of 100.

Kazakhstan (Population 18.2 M, rank 64, growth 1.2%. Not free: 22 of 100. Area 2.72 M km^2, rank 9.).

Armenia: (Population 2.9 M, rank 138, growth 0.2%. Partly free: 45 of 100).

Azerbaijan: (Population 9.8 M, rank 90, growth 1.1%. Not free 14 of 100).

Uzbekistan: (Population 31.9 M, rank 44, growth 1.5%. Not free: 3 of 100).

Kyrgyzstan (Population 6 M, rank 112, growth 1.5%. Partly free, 37 of 100).

Tajikistan: (Population 8.9 M, rank 96, growth 2.1%. Not free, 11 of 100).

Turkmenistan: (Population 5.7 M, rank 113, growth 1.7%. Not free, 4 of 100).

United Kingdom, Canada, South America

United Kingdom: (Population: 66.1 M, rank 21, growth 0.6%. Free: 95 of 100).

2 April 2020. Reports: A London-based company has been contracted to build OxVent Ventilators, which are the result of a collaboration with scientists, clinicians, and medical technology manufacturers from the University of Oxford, King's College London and Smith+Nephew.

7 April 2020. Reports: British Prime Minister Boris Johnson received oxygen support overnight, but was not put on a ventilator, after being moved to intensive care, as his coronavirus symptoms worsened. Foreign Secretary Dominic Raab is taking the helm for the time being, in the latest turn in Brexit developments.

8 April 2020. Vladimir Putin sent a message to Prime Minister of Great Britain Boris Johnson.

The message reads, in part: "I would like to express my sincere support in this difficult moment. I am confident that your energy, optimism and sense of humor will help you defeat the illness."

The President of Russia wished Boris Johnson a quick and full recovery.

12 April 2020. PM health update. A statement from Downing Street. The PM has been discharged from hospital to continue his recovery, at Chequers.

On the advice of his medical team, the PM will not be immediately returning to work. He wishes to thank everybody at St Thomas' for the brilliant care he has received.

All of his thoughts are with those affected by this illness.

27 April 2020. Prime Minister Boris Johnson made a statement in Downing Street, starting with "I am sorry I have been away from my desk for much longer than I would have liked, and I want to thank everybody who has stepped up."

Ireland: (Population: 4.7 M, rank 123, growth 0.8%. Free: 96 of 100)

Canada: (Population: 36.6 M, rank 38, growth 0.9%. Free: 99 of 100. Area 9.9 M km^2, rank 2).

<u>Iceland</u>: (Population: 335,000, rank 180, growth 0.8%. Free 97 of 100).

<u>Mexico</u>: (Population: 129.1 M, rank 10, growth 1.3%. Partly Free: 65 of 100. Area 1.96 M km^2, rank 13).

<u>Chile</u>: (Population: 18 M, rank 65, growth 0.8%. Free 94 of 100).

Reports: Chilean food processing sector represents 25% of the country's economy, with annual sales of $34 billions. The Chilean food sector is the second most important sector in the country, after mining. Chile enjoys a robust commercial network, thanks to its 29 trade agreements with 65 countries.

<u>Colombia</u>: (Population: 49 M, rank 29, growth 0.8%. Partly free 64 of 100).

Reports: Colombian raw sugar production is estimated to slightly decrease to 2.35 millions of metric tons (MMT) in marketing year (MY) 2019/2020, with no changes in MY 2020/21.

<u>Argentina</u>: (Population: 44.2 M, rank 31, growth, 1%. Free: 82 of 100. Area 2.78 M km^2, rank 8.).

Reports: Argentine imports of consumer-oriented food and beverages in 2020 are projected to remain at 2019 levels, because of the continuing economic uncertainty, weak consumer spending, and the expectation of high inflation.

<u>Brazil</u> (Population: 209.2 M, rank 6, growth 0.8%. Free, 79 of 100. Area 8.5 M km^2, rank 5).

<u>Ecuador</u>: (Population: 17.3 M, rank 67, growth 1.7%. Partly free: 57 of 100)

<u>Peru</u>: (Population: 32.1 M, rank 5, growth 1.2%. Free: 72 of 100)

<u>Cuba</u>: (Population: 11.4 M, rank 42, growth 0.1%. Not free, 15 of 100).

Bolivia: (Population: 11 M, rank 83, growth 1.5%. Partly free 68 of 100).

Paraguay: (Population: 6.8 M, rank 107, growth 1.3%. Partly free 64 of 100).

Panama: (Population: 4.1 M, rank 131, growth 1.6%. Free: 83 of 100).

Venezuela: (Population: 32 M, rank 43, growth 1.3%. Not free: 30 of 100).

20 April 2020. Vladimir Putin had a telephone conversation with President of the Bolivarian Republic of Venezuela, Nicolas Maduro, at the initiative of the Venezuelan side.

Issues regarding the fight against the spread of the coronavirus were discussed. Nicolas Maduro expressed gratitude for the assistance rendered by Russia including a supply of test systems.

The leaders stressed the importance of coordinated steps by the international community to fight this new global threat including the implementation of Vladimir Putin's initiative on setting up "green corridors" free from trade wars and sanctions to supply medications, food, equipment and technologies, for the duration of the crisis.

As the parties shared opinions on developments in the global oil market, they stressed the great importance of the agreement reached by OPEC+ on the coordinated reduction of oil production.

Current issues of furthering the Russian-Venezuelan strategic partnership were touched upon, primarily in trade and the economy. Russia reaffirmed its support for efforts by Venezuela's legitimate government to settle the domestic political discord via a nation-wide dialogue. The leaders emphasized the unacceptability of destructive external interference in Venezuela's affairs.

It was agreed to maintain contacts at various levels including the respective health ministries.

Guyana: (Population 777K, (rank 165, grows 0.6%). Free: 74 of 100).

Trinidad and Tobago: (Population 1.3 M, (rank 153, grows 0.3%). Free: 81 of 100).

Nicaragua: (Population 6.2 M, (rank 110, grows 1.1%). Partly Free: 47 of 100).

El Salvador: (Population 6.3 M (rank 108, grows 0.5%). Free: 70 of 100).

France, Paris (250 BC): l'Hôtel de Ville (City Hall since 1357, King Francis I started this building in 1533, finished 1628, 1873-1892

France, Germany, and neighbors

France: (Population 64.9 M, rank 22, growth 0.4%. Free: 90 of 100).

17 April 2020. Vladimir Putin had a telephone conversation with President of the French Republic, Emmanuel Macron, on the French side's initiative. The two presidents exchanged opinions on the situation concerning the spread of the coronavirus pandemic and informed each other about the measures being undertaken in Russia and France to minimize, among other things, unfavorable socioeconomic effects. Emmanuel Macron expressed gratitude for the assistance with returning French nationals home as well as for help in creating conditions for the transit of medications and medical equipment across Russia to France.

The parties expressed their intent to preserve the dynamics in the development of bilateral cooperation and noted the importance of the contact established between the leaders of the two countries.

The possibility of organizing a working meeting of leaders of the UN Security Council's permanent members via videoconference was also discussed.

Other issues on the international agenda, including settlement of the internal Ukrainian conflict were also touched upon.

Reports: The Make Our Planet Great Again initiative, launched by Emmanuel Macron, is conducted by both the French Ministry for Foreign Affairs and Campus France.

People say that, unfortunately, our Planet was never great, because had wars all the time – it is time to start working on peace, good health and prosperity.

Belgium (Population 11.4 M, rank 80, growth 0.6%. Free: 95 of 100).

European Commission, European Union, EU: 28 EU countries: Austria, Belgium, Bulgaria, Croatia, Republic of Cyprus, Czech Republic, Denmark, Estonia, Finland, France, Germany, Greece, Hungary, Ireland, Italy, Latvia, Lithuania, Luxembourg, Malta, Netherlands, Poland, Portugal, Romania, Slovakia, Slovenia, Spain, Sweden and the UK.

NATO 29 member states: Albania, Belgium, Bulgaria, Canada, Croatia, Czech Republic, Denmark, Estonia, France, Germany, Greece, Hungary, Iceland, Italy, Latvia, Lithuania, Luxembourg, Montenegro, Netherlands, Norway, Poland, Portugal, Romania, Slovakia, Slovenia, Spain, Turkey, United Kingdom, and United States

NATO was created in 1949 with 12 states, and now includes 29 countries. The aggregate war-related expenses of its members exceed 70% of the world's total war-related spending.

Germany: (Population 82.1 M, rank 16, growth 0.2%. Free: 95 of 100).

An Erlangen, Germany-based company said its Fast Track Diagnostics (FTD) SARS-COV-2 Assay is already being shipped in Europe for research use only. Siemens Healthineers is looking at speaking with FDA to release the test under Emergency Use Authorization.

22 April 2020. Vladimir Putin had a telephone conversation with Federal Chancellor of the Federal Republic of Germany, Angela Merkel, at the German side's initiative.

The discussion focused on countering the coronavirus pandemic. The two leaders stressed the importance of closely coordinated international efforts in this area with the active involvement of the World Health Organization. They agreed to maintain bilateral contacts between relevant ministries.

The settlement of the intra-Ukrainian conflict was discussed in detail. The two leaders praised the recent prisoner exchange between Kiev and the Donetsk and Lugansk people's republics. They emphasized that consistent implementation of the Minsk Package of Measures, and decisions made at the Normandy format summit was necessary. It was noted, in particular, that the Ukrainian authorities should fulfil their commitments regarding the political aspect of the settlement process, including the formalization of the special status of Donbass in Ukrainian law.

The two leaders also touched upon the developments in Syria and Libya, as well as the current situation on the global oil market.

Norway (Population 5.3 M, rank 118, growth 1%. Free: 100 of 100).

Sweden (Population 9.9 M, rank 89, growth 0.7%. Free: 100 of 100).

The Netherlands (Population 17 M, rank 67, growth 0.3%. Free: 99 of 100).

Czech Republic (Population 10.6 M, rank 87, growth 0.1%. Free: 94 of 100).

1 May 2020. Xinhua: Chinese President Xi Jinping said on Thursday, 30 April, that China firmly supports the Czech Republic's fight against COVID-19.

Xi told Czech President Milos Zeman in a telephone conversation that China is ready to share coronavirus containment information and experience with the Czech side via bilateral channels, and the mechanism for cooperation between China and Central and Eastern European countries (CEECs), among others. Xi said that China has made arduous efforts and achieved important strategic achievement in combating the COVID-19 epidemic, noting that it is pushing for a nationwide resumption of work and production while keeping up with the efforts in epidemic prevention and control.

Xi recalled that at the critical time when the Chinese people were making an all-out effort to battle the outbreak, President Zeman called on all walks of life in the Czech society to donate money or goods, and dispatched a flight to send anti-epidemic supplies to China, demonstrating true friendship towards the Chinese people.

The Chinese leader stressed that the human race is a community with a shared future that goes through thick and thin together, particularly when facing a pandemic, adding that China is willing to work with the Czech Republic, and the wider international community, to actively implement joint prevention and control measures to contain the spread of the virus, and strengthen macroeconomic policy coordination at the same time, so as to jointly tackle the challenges to the global economy brought by the COVID-19 outbreak, and firmly safeguard international equity and justice, as well as the basic norms of international relations. Xi said he believes that with the concerted efforts by the international community, the human kind will eventually defeat the disease.

On the bilateral relationship, Xi said its sound development is in the fundamental interests of the two countries and the two peoples.

China attaches great importance to developing its ties with the Czech Republic and is willing to work together with the Czech side to constantly boost their strategic partnership, he added.

Xi also said he is looking forward to meeting with Zeman after the COVID-19 pandemic is over, to jointly plan for the future of China's relations with the Czech Republic and the CEECs.

Zeman, for his part, said that China has successfully brought the novel coronavirus epidemic under control and its economy has shown good prospects for development.

While expressing gratitude to China for providing valuable support and assistance to the Czech Republic in fighting the epidemic, he said that the friendship between the two countries is deep-rooted, and the two peoples share friendly feelings towards each other.

Zeman said that as a sincere friend of China, he will make great efforts to promote bilateral cooperation, to ensure that the relations between the two countries will ward off distractions and keep moving forward. He added that he looks forward to visiting China again soon.

Denmark (Population 5.7 M, rank 114, growth 0.4%. Free: 97 of 100. Area (including Greenland) 2.22 M km^2, rank 12 but not official).

Luxembourg (Population 583 K, rank 169, growth 1.3%. Free: 98 of 100).

Spain: (Population 46.3 M, rank 30, growth 0%. Free: 94 of 100).

Portugal: (Population 10.3 M, rank 88, decrease 0.4%. Free: 97 of 100).

Liechtenstein: (Population: 38,000, rank 215, growth 0.7%, Free: 91 of 100)

India, Pakistan, Australia, and neighbors

India (Population: 1.3 B, rank 2nd, growth 1.1%. Free: 77 of 100. Area 3.28 M km^2, rank 7).

Reports: India is considering restarting some of its manufacturing this week, even if the world's biggest lockdown is extended to the end of the month, as is expected. That lockdown is to end Tuesday, 14 April, and Prime Minister Modi has directed that some crucial industries get going again as soon as Wednesday, 15 April, Reuters reports. Separately, the industries ministry has recommended restarting manufacturing in autos, textiles, defense, electronics and other sectors.

14 April 2020. Reports: India is extending the world's biggest 1.3 B people pandemic lockdown at least until May 3. The country's restrictions were set to end today, even as its confirmed case count crossed 10,000 and deaths hit 339 (low numbers compared to harder-hit countries, which experts caution may be due to low testing levels). Despite the extension of the restrictions, India has expressed an interest in at least partially restarting its manufacturing industry now rather than later.

Reports: The Indian government has extended the March 25th national lockdown until May 3rd.

Indonesia: (Population: 263.9 M, rank 4, growth 1.1%. Partly free: 65 of 100. Area 1.91 M km^2, rank 14.).

12 April 2020. Vladimir Putin had a telephone conversation with President of the Republic of Indonesia, Joko Widodo, at the Indonesian side's initiative. When discussing the coronavirus pandemic, the two presidents confirmed their intention for close cooperation in the fight against the infection, and agreed, in particular, to step up contacts between the healthcare ministries of Russia and Indonesia. Current issues of developing bilateral cooperation in other areas was also touched upon.

Australia: (Population: 24.4 M, rank 53, growth 1.3%. Free: 98 of 100. Area 7.69 M km^2, rank 6).

8 April 2020. Reports: Australia has become the first, of 11 nations rated "AAA" by S&P, to have been put on negative outlook since the coronavirus outbreak.

New Zealand: (Population 4.7 M, rank 125, growth 1%. Free: 98 of 100.

Pakistan: (Population 212 M, rank 5, growth 2%. Partly free: 43 of 100).

Philippines: (Population 104.9 M, rank 13, growth 1.5%. Partly free 63 of 100).

Singapore: (Population 5.7 M, rank 115, growth 1.5%. Partly free 51 of 100).

The EAS currently comprises 18 countries: 10 ASEAN members (Brunei Darussalam, Cambodia, Indonesia, Laos, Malaysia, Myanmar, the Philippines, Singapore, Thailand and Vietnam), and eight dialogue partners: Russia (joined the EAS in 2010), the United States, Japan, South Korea, India, China, Australia and New Zealand.

APEC (21 members: Singapore, China, USA, Vietnam, Australia, Japan, Indonesia, Russia, Philippines, Malaysia, Hong Kong, Thailand, Chile, Canada, New Zealand, South Korea, Peru, Mexico, Brunei, Papua New Guinea, Chinese Taipei)

Thailand: (Population 69 M, rank 20, growth 0.3%. Not free 32 of 100).

Reports: Rice export prices declined 6% as foreign buyers reportedly sought Vietnamese rice, after the government resumed rice exports.

Myanmar (Burma, Population 53.3 M, rank 26, growth 0.9%. Not free 32 of 100.

Bangladesh (Population 164.6 M, rank 8, growth 1.1%. Partly free 47 of 100).

Reports: For market year (MY) 2020 -2021 (May-April), Post forecasts Bangladesh's rice production to increase, assuming favorable weather and increased yield. Rice imports are expected to increase.

Sri Lanka (Population 20.8 M, rank 58, growth 0.4%. Partly free 56 of 100).

Reports: Government of Sri Lanka has notified temporary suspension of import of commodities from April 16 to July 15, 2020.

Malaysia (Population 31.6 M, rank 45, growth 1.34%. Partly free 44 of 100).

Brunei: (Population 428,000, rank 176, growth 1.3%. Not free 29 of 100).

Vanuatu: (Population 276,000, rank 185, growth 2.2%. Free 80 of 100)

Tonga: (Population 108,000, rank 195, growth 0.8%. Free 74 of 100

Papua New Guinea: (Population 8.2 M, rank 101, growth 2.1%, Partly Free 64 of 100).

Italy, Middle East, Africa

Italy: (Population 59.3 M, rank 23, decrease 0.1%. Free: 89 of 100).

Vatican: (Population 792, rank 233 (last), decrease 1.1%).

San Marino: (Population 33,400, rank 218, growth 0.6%. Free 97 of 100)

Malta (Population 431,000, rank 175, growth 0.3%. Free, 96 of 100).

Jordan (Population 9.7 M, rank 92, growth 2.6%. Partly free, 37 of 100).

Lebanon: (Population: 6 M, rank 111, growth 1.3%. Partly free: 44 of 100).
Reports: Chinese military had sent medical supplies and experts to many countries, including Iran, Pakistan, Myanmar, Laos, Cambodia, Vietnam and Lebanon. Chinese military medical teams had also held seminars with peers from Pakistan, Singapore and Russia.

United Arab Emirates (UAE) (Population: 9.4 M, rank 94, growth 1.4%. Not free, 20 of 100. Capital: Abu Dhabi. Big city: Dubai).
Reports: FAS Dubai (Post) forecasts UAE imports of wheat, rice, corn and barley to increase in MY2020/2021.

Saudi Arabia (Population 32.9 M, rank 41, growth 2.1%. Not free: 10 of 100. Area 2.149 M km^2, rank 12.).
10 April 2020. Vladimir Putin had a telephone conversation with Crown Prince of Saudi Arabia, Mohammad bin Salman Al Saud. The sides discussed issues related to the OPEC+ talks on reducing oil production, and agreed on further Russian-Saudi contacts in this context.

12 April 2020. Telephone conversations with Donald Trump and Salman bin Abdulaziz Al Saud. Vladimir Putin had a telephone conversation with US President Donald Trump and King of Saudi Arabia Salman bin Abdulaziz Al Saud. The leaders confirmed the agreement reached within OPEC+ to voluntarily and gradually cut oil production in order to stabilize the global markets, and ensure the sustainability of the global economy in general. This agreement is about to come into force. Vladimir Putin also had a separate telephone conversation with Donald Trump. The two leaders again exchanged opinions on the developments on the global oil markets, and noted the importance of the OPEC+ deal to reduce production. Current issues of ensuring strategic security were also discussed.
Vladimir Putin wished Donald Trump and all Christians in America a happy Easter. It was agreed to maintain contacts between the leaders of the Russian Federation, the United States of America, and the Kingdom of Saudi Arabia.

Yemen (Population 28.2 M, rank 50, growth 2.4%. Not free: 14 of 100).

Iraq (Population 38.2 M, rank 36, growth 2.9%. Not free: 27 of 100).

Iran: (Population 81.1 M, rank 18, growth 1.1%. Not free: 17 of 100).

21 April 2020. Vladimir Putin had a telephone conversation with President of the Islamic Republic of Iran, Hassan Rouhani.
The presidents discussed countering the spread of the coronavirus infection. In this context, Hassan Rouhani thanked Russia for its assistance to Iran. It was agreed to step up cooperation between relevant departments, including direct contacts between the healthcare ministries. The leaders emphasized the importance of consolidating the efforts of the international community to fight the coronavirus pandemic, as well as the Russian initiative to create "green corridors" during the crisis for unhindered supplies of medications, equipment and technology and to introduce a moratorium on any restrictions on exports of essential goods.

The presidents also reviewed a number of urgent issues of bilateral cooperation, including the implementation of major joint projects in energy, agriculture and transport.

While exchanging views on the situation in Syria, the leaders expressed the shared intention to continue cooperation with a view to reaching a long-term settlement in that country, primarily in the Astana format, which has proven effective.

Israel: (Population 8.3 M, rank 100, growth 1.6%. Free: 80 of 100).

8 April 2020. Vladimir Putin had a telephone conversation with Prime Minister of Israel, Benjamin Netanyahu, at the initiative of the Israeli side.

The parties discussed topical issues of bilateral relations. They expressed a mutual stance in favor of enhancing coordination in countering the spread of the coronavirus infection. Vladimir Putin congratulated Benjamin Netanyahu on the coming holiday of Passover. They agreed on contacts at various levels.

Palestine: (Population 4.9 M (rank 121, grows 2.7%). Not free: 28 of 100).

Egypt (Population 97.5 M (rank 14, grows 1.9%). Not free, 26 of 100).

League of Arab States (LAS) (22 countries: Algeria, Bahrein, Comoros, Djibouti, Egypt, Iraq, Jordan, Kuwait, Lebanon, Libya, Mauritania, Morocco, Oman, Palestine, Qatar, Saudi Arabia, Somalia, Sudan, Syria, Tunisia, United Arab Emirates and Yemen).

Qatar: (Population 2.6 M (rank 142, grows 2.7%). Not free: 26 of 100).

Kuwait: (Population 4.1 M (rank 130, grows 2.1%). Partly free: 36 of 100).

Oman: (Population 4.6 M (rank 127, grows 4.8%). Not free: 25 of 100)

Bahrain: (Population 1.5 M (rank 152, grows 4.7%). Not free: 12 of 100).

Syria: (Population 18.2 M (rank 63, decrease 0.9%). Not free: 0 of 100).

Kenya: (Population 49.7 M (rank 28, growth 2.6%. Partly free, 51 of 100).

Libya: (Population 6.3 M, rank 109, growth 1.3%. Not free: 13 of 100).

Algeria: (Population 41.3 M, rank 34, growth 1.8%. Partly Free 35 of 100. Area 2.38 M km^2, rank 10.)

Tunisia: (Population 11.5 M, rank 78, growth 1.1%. Free: 78 of 100).

Morocco: (Population 35.7 M, rank 39, growth 1.3%. Partly free: 41 of 100).

South Africa: (Population 56.7 M, rank 25, growth 1.3%. Free, 78 of 100).

2 April 2020. Vladimir Putin had a telephone conversation with President of South Africa, Cyril Ramaphosa, at the South African side's initiative.

The presidents discussed possible cooperation in countering the coronavirus pandemic and its consequences, including considering the results of the recent G20 virtual summit. As President of the country chairing the African Union, Cyril Ramaphosa gave an update on the steps the organization planned to take.

The two leaders agreed to coordinate efforts to bring home Russian citizens from South Africa.

Zimbabwe: (Population 16.5 M, rank 70, growth 2.4%. Partly Free, 32 of 100).

Sudan (Population 40.5 M, rank 35, growth 2.4%. Not Free: 6 of 100).

South Sudan (Population 12.5 M, rank 76, growth 2.8%. Not Free: 4 of 100)

Guinea: (Population 12.7 M, rank 75, growth 2.6%. Partly Free, 41 of 100).

Djibouti (Population 957,000, rank 160, growth 1.6%. Not Free: 26 of 100).

Somalia: (Population 14.7 M, rank 74, growth 3%. Not free: 5 of 100).

Niger (Population 21.4 M, rank 57, growth 3.9%. Partly free: 49 of 100).

Nigeria (Population 190.8 M, rank 7, growth 2.6%. Partly free: 50 of 100).

Cameroon (Population 24 M, rank 55, growth 2.6%. Not free: 24 of 100).

Sierra Leone: (Population 7.5 M (rank 103, grows 2.2%). Partly free: 66 of 100)

Chad: (Population 15 M (rank 73, grows 3.1%). Not free: 18 of 100).

The Gambia: (Population 2.1 M (rank 146, grows 3%). Not free: 20 of 100).

Malawi: (Population 18.6 M (rank 61, grows 2.9%). Partly free: 63 of 100).

Rwanda: (Population 12.2 M (rank 77, grows 2.4%). Not free: 24 of 100).

Burkina Faso: (Population 19.1 M (rank 60, grows 2.9%). Partly free: 63 of 100).

Central African Republic: (Population 4.6 M (rank 126, grows 1.4%). Not free: 10 of 100).

Senegal: (Population 15.8 M (rank 72, grows 2.8%). Free: 78 of 100).

Gabon: (Population 2 M (rank 149, grows 2.3%). Partly Free: 32 of 100).

Madagascar: (Population 25.5 M (rank 51, grows 2.7%). Partly Free: 56 of 100).

Democratic Republic of the Congo: (Population 81.3 M (rank 17, grows 3.3%). Not Free: 19 of 100. Area 2.34 M km^2, rank 11).

Angola: (Population 29.7 M (rank 46, grows 3.4%). Not Free: 24 of 100).

Zambia: (Population 17 M (rank 66, grows 3%). Partly Free: 56 of 100).

United Republic of Tanzania: (Population 57 M (rank 24, grows 3.1%). Partly Free: 58 of 100).

Ethiopia: (Population 105 M (rank 12, grows 2.5%). Not Free: 12 of 100).

8 April 2020. Vladimir Putin had a telephone conversation with Prime Minister of the Federative Democratic Republic of Ethiopia, Abiy Ahmed, at the Ethiopian side's initiative.

While discussing the situation caused by the spread of the coronavirus, both parties stressed the importance of invigorating efforts of the entire international community, including the IMF and the World Bank, to combat the infection. They have also considered some topical aspects of developing bilateral relations.

Uganda: (Population 42.8 M (rank 33, grows 3.3%). Partly Free: 35 of 100).

Mozambique: (Population 30.3 M (rank 46, grows 2.9%). Partly Free: 53 of 100).

Namibia: (Population 2.5 M (rank 143, grows 1.9%). Free: 77 of 100).

Mauritius: (Population 1.2 M (rank 157, growth 0.8%). Free: 89 of 100).

Equatorial Guinea: (Population 1.35 M (rank 154, growth 3.6%). Not Free: 8 of 100).

Ghana: (Population 28.8 M (rank 48, growth 2.22%). Free: 83 of 100).

Côte d'Ivoire: (Population 25.7 M (rank 106, growth 2.58%). Partly Free: 51 of 100).
Reports: Milled rice production for MY 2020/21 is projected at 1.4 millions of metric tons (MMT).

Paris - The north and east sides of l'Arc de Triomphe de l'Étoile, started by Napoleon in 1806, height 50 m, wide 45 m, deep 22 m.

Medical

2 April 2020. Reports: The U.S. Department of Health and Human Services awarded a grant to San Diego, CA-based Cue Health to accelerate the development, validation, and FDA clearance of a portable, molecular diagnostic test to detect SARS-CoV-2, the virus that causes COVID-19, in less than 25 minutes, using a simple nasal swab.

Novacyt launches two-hour coronavirus test.

Researchers are working to generate libraries of lipid nanoparticles for the targeted delivery and screening of nucleic acids. The goal is to improve the therapeutic index, while reducing unwanted side effects in translational disease models.

Using vapor-phase hydrogen peroxide, a single Critical Care Decontamination System could process up to 80,000 respirator masks daily.

An Austin, TX-based company was granted Emergency Use Authorization for the Aries SARS-CoV-2 Assay, and the NxTAG CoV Extended Panel, to help in the detection of the new coronavirus.

April 7 is World Health Day.

Medical robots' role expands, as COVID-19 outbreak continues: robots are in high demand as medical professionals seek hands-free ways to disinfect environments and contain the spread of coronavirus and COVID-19.

Reports: Pandemics take place in the world about every 10 years. For example, the 1957 Asian flu, the 1967 Hong Kong flu, etc. The last pandemic took place in 2009 with the swine flu virus.

The current pandemic is a potentially serious acute viral respiratory infection. Over 80% of cases are mild, 15% are severe, and 5% are critical. The main feature is that asymptomatic carriers with no clinical presentation can pass on the virus. This is the feature that defines this entire situation.

Another important feature is that the latency period is 14 days. While flu takes 3–5 days, this infection takes 14, which is quite a long latency period.

Complications from the coronavirus infection, such as pneumonia, can be a greater threat to the patient than the infection itself.

Experts such as pulmonologists, anesthesiologists, intensive care experts, infectiologists, paediatricians, obstetrician-gynaecologists and perinatologists are ready round the clock to provide virtual or onsite consultations where needed.

The old people are the hardest hit. But almost 20% of those put on ventilators are under 45. They have chronic diseases, not only lung and cardiovascular diseases, but some are oncological patients and are receiving treatment, while others have renal failure, obesity, and type 2 diabetes, which makes proper respiratory support very difficult.

Scientists have announced a potential vaccine against SARS-CoV-2, the new coronavirus causing the COVID-19 pandemic. When tested in mice, the vaccine, delivered through a fingertip-sized patch, produces antibodies specific to SARS-CoV-2 at quantities thought to be sufficient for neutralizing the virus.

A single use, wireless biosensor patch for the early detection and monitoring of coronavirus symptoms is being fast tracked for introduction within weeks. Based on a proven cardiovascular monitoring platform, the Biosensor Patch 1AX, simply affixed on the chest, will record temperature, respiration rate, ECG trace, heart rate and movement — in real time.

Mylan announced that the production of malaria med hydroxychloroquine sulfate for COVID-19 patients, out of the company's plant in West Virginia, has advanced ahead of schedule. The company is donating 10 M doses to the U.S. Department of Health and Human Services for possible use in clinical studies, or under emergency use authorization, and making shipments to wholesalers. Meanwhile, Medtronic stated that its Puritan Bennett 560 ventilator will be available next month in the U.S. under emergency use authorization from the FDA. The company expects to be producing 1,000 ventilators per week by the end of June and projects that it will produce 25 K ventilators across all platforms over the next six months.

There are more than 200,000 US cases per year of otitis externa, which is an infection of the outer ear canal that runs from the eardrum to the outside of the head.

Reports: As clinical trials related to COVID-19 continue, the focus will start to shift on which vaccines and treatments have the best chance to make it to mass production. There has been a lot of discussion about Gilead Sciences' remdesivir, Regeneron Pharmaceuticals' cocktail antibodies, and Moderna's vaccine candidate. Other companies racing ahead with vaccine trials at various stages include BioNTech, Pfizer, Dynavax Technologies, Vaxart, GlaxoSmithKline, Heat Biologics, Inovio Pharmaceuticals, Translate Bio, Johnson & Johnson, Arcturus Therapeutics, CSL Behring and Novavax. Treatment candidates are being worked on by CalciMedica, Amgen, Adaptive Biotechnologies, Takeda Pharmaceutical, CytoDyn, Roche Holdings, Regeneron Pharmaceuticals, Tiziana Life Sciences, Vir Biotechnology, Eli Lilly, Sanofi, and others. Moderna will host its Vaccine Day on 14 April. Presentations from CEO Stéphane Bancel, Chief Medical Officer Tal Zaks, and key opinion leaders will focus on mRNA vaccines, and the company's core prophylactic vaccines modality.

Reports: Gilead Sciences' experimental drug for patients with severe COVID-19 infections showed promise in an early analysis published in The New England Journal of Medicine, raising hopes that the first treatment for the new virus may be on the horizon. A cohort analysis of 53 severely ill hospitalized COVID-19 patients who received the company's antiviral remdesivir, on a compassionate use basis, showed 68% needed less oxygen or breathing machine support. Results from more rigorous studies are expected by the end of this month.

UC Berkeley launches 'Pop-Up' COVID-19 Testing Lab in 3 weeks. UC Berkeley's robotic system has the capacity to handle over 1,000 patient samples a day.

15 April 2020. Reports: FDA issued EUA to first saliva-based coronavirus test - the test was developed by Rutgers' RUCDR Infinite Biologics and collaborators. The diagnostic uses saliva as the primary biomaterial to detect the SARS-CoV-2 coronavirus.

15 April 2020. Reports: Synapse Biomedical said its TransAeris DPS is used to assist in weaning patients determined by their healthcare provider to be at high risk of weaning failure off of ventilators, in healthcare settings during the COVID-19 pandemic for no more than 30 days.

There are several safety concerns for patients with metallic implants who require MRIs, including magnetic forces, torques, radio-frequency-induced heating, gradient-induced heating and vibrations, unintended stimulation, and device malfunction.

Abbott developed four separate tests to address this pandemic.

Specialists are looking for a thin film that, when applied to hands and other open parts of the human body, would prevent people from being infected with the COVID-19.

Roche is making coronavirus antibody tests.

FemtoDx is working to develop rapid at-home COVID-19 test.

Monash University researchers are developing a new medical device to reduce the risk of complications following a common procedure to unblock clogged arteries.

Nexletol is a daily pill approved for people with a genetic predisposition for high cholesterol, and for heart disease patients who need to further reduce their bad cholesterol.

FDA warned healthcare providers on Tuesday, 21 April, that serological tests intended to detect antibodies to SARS-CoV-2 should not be used as the sole basis to diagnose infection. Such tests would initially be available for healthcare workers and first responders, who could have been exposed to COVID-19 or might be symptomatic. In the coming weeks, LabCorp said it plans to make the at-home test available to the public.

FDA has authorized the first diagnostic test with a home collection option for COVID-19. Specifically, the FDA re-issued the emergency use authorization (EUA) for the LabCorp COVID-19 RT-PCR Test to permit testing of samples self-collected by patients at home, using LabCorp's Pixel by LabCorp COVID-19 Test home collection kit.

VisCardia is developing VisOne, an implantable system that delivers synchronized diaphragmatic stimulation (SDS) therapy for improving cardiac function.

26 April 2020. Reports: The American Association for Cancer Research AACR Virtual Annual Meeting will take place next week. The program will include a number of clinical trial plenary sessions featuring more than 30 oral presentations, along with perspectives on the science behind the clinical trials, by expert discussants.

There are a few different forms of adrenal insufficiency, but they're all caused by insufficient production of hormones from the adrenal glands.

Reports: As confirmed coronavirus cases in the U.S. top one million, Pfizer is the latest vaccine developer saying it may have a candidate ready for emergency use in the U.S. by September or October. It's another example of breathtaking development speed, potentially only 9-10 months from the publication of the genetic sequence of the SARS-CoV-2 virus in January, to vaccine availability, a process that usually takes at least 10 years. Sanofi, GlaxoSmithKline, and Johnson & Johnson are all working intensily to generate clinical data, and ramp up production to meet huge global demand.

Current Health is launching a collaboration with Mayo Clinic to develop monitoring solutions with AI, that accelerate the identification of COVID-19 patients and predict symptom and disease severity.

Moderna's experimental vaccine, mRNA-1273, is currently being tested in early-stage trial by the US. National Institutes of Health, with mid-stage trials set for Q2. The 10-year collaboration agreement will see the companies produce up to a billion vaccine doses per year at Lonza U.S., and would cover additional products in the future. In April, Moderna had $483 M in U.S. federal funding to accelerate development of mRNA-1273.

Italy, Venezia - Piazza San Marco with Palazzo Ducale (right), Libreria Sansoviniana (next to Palazzo Ducale), Basilica di San Marco (back), Giardini Reali and Il Campanile (center-right), Procuratie Nuove (center to left), Capitano di Porto (left).

Mathematics, Science, Technology, AI, Space

The newest edition of NASA's small, foldable robots will scout regions on the Moon, and gain information about locations that may be difficult for astronauts to investigate on foot. Small enough to fit in a shoebox, multiple robots can be deployed to work together, and collaborate on their task.

New self-charging battery for electronic devices: the cell, developed by collaborators in the U.S. and Portugal, combines negative capacitance and negative resistance to recharge without losing power.

Collaboration uses AI to expand medical imaging services: Nanox is onboarding key players in the artificial intelligence space to help improve the accessibility and affordability of early-detection services. The latest collaboration is with Qure.ai.

Collaborative robots have a great future.

Histology images hold great potential as a resource for target and biomarker discovery activities. However, in order to use such complex phenotypic data, it is necessary that strong image analysis tools are developed. Researchers are working on an image analysis mathematical algorithm for the good segmentation of histology sections.

Reports: Apple and Google have unveiled a rare partnership to add technology to their smartphone platforms that will alert users if they have come into contact with a person with COVID-19. The companies announced jointly on Friday, 10 April, that the "contact tracing" tools they are developing would be built into smartphones, using existing Bluetooth technology that tracks whether phones have passed within a certain distance of one another. Users then could be alerted if they were in contact with an infected person.

People must opt in to the system, but it has the potential to monitor about a third of the world's population.

AI-powered CT imaging system shown to detect COVID-19 - study shows that RADLogics's system can automatically and accurately detect COVID-19, and quantify the disease burden in patients.

Sano has developed a biometric sensor that can tell people important things about their health, by revealing how the person's body metabolizes glucose – it is useful in telemedicine.

A new tool for medical professionals may help shed more light on tumors in the body, and how the brain operates. Purdue University researchers created technology that uses optical imaging to better help surgeons map out tumors in the body, and help them understand how certain diseases affect activity in the brain.

Engineers work to remove nanoscale organic contamination, and increase hydrophilicity of surfaces with complex geometries, without affecting the bulk material properties. They apply plasma treatment to a broad range of materials for microfluidics and solar cell research, cell culturing, and biomedical applications.

Over the years the role of Artificial Intelligence (AI) in medicine has become increasingly important. A growing number of disciplines and branches of medicine are using AI in some capacity or other; they include radiology, genomics, oncology and cardiology, to name a few. AI assists researchers to solve complex problems that would otherwise be difficult.

Healx deploys AI drug discovery technology against rare nerve disease.

Researchers are looking for innovative ideas that can integrate renewable energy sources (RES) with gas power plants (GPP), necessary to ensure the adequacy of the energy system in the transitioning phase towards more renewable energy generation.

For the first time, a robotic spacecraft caught an old satellite and extended its life.

Power-beaming was demonstrated on International Space Station - researchers at an U.S. Research Laboratory are investigating space solar and power beaming, as a potential source of clean energy for a variety of civilian applications.

Researchers have developed an artificial intelligence-based system that can listen to a cough, and look for signs of COVID-19.

In response to increasing demand for sensors that are used to make ventilators, Sensirion has launched a new flow sensor that has been optimized for respiratory applications, and is available in high volumes.

Knowing the air density outside a spacecraft can have a substantial effect on its ability to hit a specific landing spot. A new onboard mathematical algorithm provides real-time data to aid in steering the craft, particularly during the crucial entry, descent, and landing stage.

Creep is the natural tendency of a material to gradually move or permanently deform as a result of mechanical stress or strain. For materials operating in high-performance systems, such as jet engines, creep can be a significant issue. But engineers found ways to alleviate this issue.

Academics from University College London are working with artificial intelligence (AI) firm Causaly, to help accelerate various aspects of research into the COVID-19 pandemic, including identification of biomarkers and potential therapeutic agents.

Renesas has introduced a new open-source ventilator system reference design that customers can use to quickly design ready-to-assemble boards for medical ventilators. Many regions are experiencing a critical shortage of ventilators as COVID-19 infections continue to rise and hospital demand exceeds supply.

Blockchain (a time-stamped growing list of immutable, transparent and decentralized records of data (which is called a block) that is distributed and managed by a cluster of computers, which links this block to others using cryptography) technology schemes are being developed by companies, like IBM and Ernst & Young, to help with different aspects of the coronavirus pandemic. The projects can be an efficient way of connecting healthcare providers in need of medical equipment, or help validate a person's immunity. Programs could have problems if the data that go on the blockchain are inaccurate and difficult to verify.

Specialists noticed that the immediate environment around a car is often ignored, and this is where ultrasonic sensor systems come into play.

Penn Engineering researchers have introduced a "metal-air scavenger" vehicle, which gets energy not from a battery, but from breaking chemical bonds in the aluminum surface it travels over. The technology, which works like both a battery and an energy harvester, has 13 times more energy density than lithium-ion batteries.

Specialists are working on efficient and cost-effective technology to remove potassium from reaction mixtures in the production of polyether polyols. The technology should be low energy consumption and produce minimal waste.

Researchers are working on non-destructive techniques to automatically detect small surfaced or partially buried archaeological finds (e.g. potsherds, lithic tools, bones, etc.) scattered in large areas, in order to improve efficiency and effectiveness of archaeological surveys, carried out during the preliminary phases of construction projects, to preserve the historical and cultural heritage.

Specialists are working on new mask designs and technologies, as well as new ideas for personal protective equipment (PPE), to prevent the transmission of respiratory viruses such as coronavirus.

General news and issues

Amazon said it will begin placing new grocery delivery customers on a wait list, and reduce shopping hours at some Whole Foods stores, to prioritize orders from existing customers buying food online during the coronavirus outbreak. Many shoppers, seeking to purchase groceries from Amazon recently, have found they could not place orders, due to a lack of available delivery slots, so the company said it will relegate all new online grocery customers to a wait list, while it works to add capacity. Amazon also plans to shorten public hours at some Whole Foods stores, so employees can more quickly fulfill online grocery orders.

The most common types of scams used by cybercriminals will target people through fake e-mails, text messages, calls, letters, or even someone showing up at their front door.

Over 80% of web traffic is encrypted, and cybercriminals increasingly are using encryption to try to hide their attacks.

Again, people are concerned about the abuses (abusers make millions of dollars) against the victims of cybercriminals, while the cybercriminals are left to continue their crimes (for the benefit of the abusers).

Criminals are taking advantage of the Covid-19 pandemic to target businesses. Not only are they using phishing scams and fake websites to spread ransomware or steal information — they're leveraging the security flaws inherent in many remote workforces to increase their criminal activity.

People ask again the authorities to arrest the cybercriminals.

Starting in May, UPS will begin using drones to fill prescriptions for residents of The Villages in Florida, one of the country's biggest retirement communities, with 135,000 residents. The deliveries will be dropped at a central location from a CVS (NYSE:CVS) store about a half mile away and an employee will then ferry them to homes via golf cart. The ultimate goal is for the program to make the deliveries directly, with the drone lowering packages by winch.

Reports: Amazon said it would spend second-quarter profits - estimated to be $4 B (under normal circumstances) - on responding to the COVID-19 pandemic. "If you're a shareowner in Amazon, you may want to take a seat, because we're not thinking small," Jeff Bezos said in an earnings release. AWS quarterly revenue topped $10 B for the first time ever.

USA, Boston Harbor (founded in 1630), in 2009: visiting tall ships from many countries, at the Boston Fish Pier (opened in 1915).

Aphorisms

Best path forward always comes from mathematics.

Italy, Roma - Arco di Tito (Arch of Titus, 82 AD, restored in 1821, left), and the church Santa Francesca Romana (975 – 1615, right).

Humor

Two old men meet near the Pacific Ocean.
The older one:
- "You, kid, put your mask!"
- "After you, sir!", responds the younger one.
- "And stay 2 meters away!"
- "But of course – tell me, old man, how is hell now?"
- "Empty!"
- "And where are all the devils?"
- "Here!"

Japan, north-west of the Sendai Station (1887), on Ekimae Dori, the restaurant Rigoletto, named after the famous opera with the same name, by Giuseppe Verdi (1813 – 1901), who wrote 37 operas, Rigoletto being the 17th, with the premiere at Teatro La Fenice, Venezia, on 11 March 1851.

Our Future is Sustainable Peace and Prosperity

For more details please see the book with the same title (number 88 in bibliography), and the following books.

All people on Earth are very concerned about these very bad facts: advanced technology for nuclear attacks, AI for war, on the future battlefield for space force, new weapons for offensive nuclear attack, EMP weapons, streams of microwaves, electromagnetic railguns, and high-power lasers, unmanned surface warships, advanced supercomputing for use in war, militarization of civilian helicopters, high-tech secret weapon to win the next big war (an impossibility, because everything would be destroyed), new low-yield nuclear missile, war exercises are continuing, new mine warfare technology. All people say that this is wrong.

Surprise medical bills and government price controls will completely disappear under the new world management.

All people ask to:
Replace smart munitions with smart books.
Replace nuclear missiles with nuclear electricity generators for all people.
Replace attack helicopters with emergency assistance helicopters for all people.
Replace combat aircraft with passenger aircraft.
Replace aviation strike planning with aviation people assistance planning.
Replace AI mathematical algorithms for war with AI mathematical algorithms for peace, good health and prosperity.

Universe Axioms

Formulated by Michael M. Dediu

The following axioms are not independent of each other. They express in different ways the same concept of infinity.

Axiom 1. Pointing a theoretical laser from Earth, in any direction, at any time, after a finite amount of time the laser beam will touch an astronomic body.

Axiom 2. In any direction in space starting from Earth, at any time, there is an astronomic body from which the Earth can be theoretically seen.

Axiom 3. Infinity of space: Any straight line passing through the Earth's center intersects an infinite number of astronomic bodies.

Axiom 4. Infinity of time: Representing the time on a line, with the origin at the beginning of the year 1, the time goes to infinite in both positive and negative directions.

Axiom 5. Infinity of life: Because of the infinity of space and time, it is normal to consider that the life exists at any time, in an infinite number of places. Therefore, right now, when you are reading this book, there is life outside the Earth, in an infinite number of places, but we do not know yet how to contact them.

Axiom 6. The Earth rotates itself around its polar axis, the Moon and many artificial satellites rotate around the Earth, in the Solar System all the planets and many other objects rotate around the Sun, the Solar System itself rotates around the center of the Milky Way galaxy, the Milky Way galaxy and all the billions of galaxies in our Universe (denoted U_1) rotate around the center of our Universe U_1, our Universe U_1, together with billions of other similar Universes, are inside a bigger Universe U_2 and rotate around the center of U_2, then U_2 and many others like it are inside a bigger U_3 and rotate around the center of U_3, and so on. Therefore, in general, the Universe U_n together with many similar Universes are inside the bigger Universe U_{n+1} and rotate around the center of U_{n+1}, for any n natural number, which goes to infinity. This can be written in the formula:

$$U_1 \subset U_2 \subset U_3 \subset \ldots \subset U_n \subset U_{n+1} \subset \ldots, \text{ n natural number.}$$

UK, Oxford, Oriel College (1326, in the east range of First quadrangle, the ornate portico in the center, with the inscription Regnante Carolo).

Time Axioms

Formulated by Michael M. Dediu

Axiom 1. Time is the most important force in the Univers.

Axiom 2. Everything is a function of time.

Axiom 3. Time exists in absolutely everything.

Axiom 4. Time creates and distroys everything.

Axiom 5. Time is invisible, inodor, insipid, unpalpabil, unaudible, but exists evrywhere.

Axiom 6. There are infinitezimal time particles, without mass, which are present everywhere, and which actually continuously transform everything.

UK, Cambridge, From Trinity Lane looking south to the west part of the northern façade and entrance of King's College Chapel (1446).

Bibliography

"The Histories" by Polybius

"Discours de la Méthode" by René Descartes

"Meditationes de prima philosophia" by René Descartes

"Philosophiae Naturalis Principia Mathematica" by Isaac Newton

Chinese encyclopedia Gujin Tushu Jicheng (Imperial Encyclopedia)

"Encyclopédie" by Jean-Baptiste le Rond d'Alembert and Denis Diderot

"Encyclopaedia Britannica" by over 4,400 contributors

"Encyclopedia Americana" by Francis Lieber

Other sources include: UPI, CNBC, AP, Nasdaq, Reuters, EDGAR, AFP, Recode, Europa Press, Bloomberg News, Fox News, USA, Deutsche Presse-Agentur, MSNBC, BBC, Australian Associated Press, Agência Brasil, The Canadian Press (La Presse Canadienne), Middle East News Agency, Baltic News Service, Suomen Tietotoimisto, Athens-Macedonian News Agency, Asian News International, Inter Press Service, Kyodo News, Notimex, Algemeen Nederlands Persbureau, AGERPRES, Newsis, Tidningarnas Telegrambyrå, Swiss Telegraphic Agency, Central News Agency, ANKA news agency, Agenzia Fides

Michael M. Dediu is also the author of these books (which can be found on Amazon.com, and www.derc.com):

1. Aphorisms and quotations – with examples and explanations
2. Axioms, aphorisms and quotations – with examples and explanations
3. 100 Great Personalities and their Quotations
4. Professor Petre P. Teodorescu – A Great Mathematician and Engineer
5. Professor Ioan Goia – A Dedicated Engineering Professor
6. Venice (Venezia) – a new perspective. A short presentation with photographs
7. La Serenissima (Venice) - a new photographic perspective. A short presentation with many photos
8. Grand Canal – Venice. A new photographic viewpoint. A short presentation with many photos

9. Piazza San Marco – Venice. A different photographic view. A short presentation with many photos

10. Roma (Rome) - La Città Eterna. A new photographic view. A short presentation with many photos

11. Why is Rome so Fascinating? A short presentation with many photos

12. Rome, Boston and Helsinki. A short photographic presentation

13. Rome and Tokyo – two captivating cities. A short photographic presentation

14. Beautiful Places on Earth – A new photographic presentation

15. From Niagara Falls to Mount Fuji via Rome - A novel photographic presentation

16. From the USA and Canada to Italy and Japan - A fresh photographic presentation

17. Paris – Why So Many Call This City Mon Amour - A lovely photographic presentation

18. The City of Light – Paris (La Ville-Lumière) - A kaleidoscopic photographic presentation

19. Paris (Lutetia Parisiorum) – the romance capital of the world - A kaleidoscopic photographic view

20. Paris and Tokyo – a joyful photographic presentation. With a preamble about the Universe

21. From USA to Japan via Canada – A cheerful photographic documentary

22. 200 Wonderful Places, In The Last 50 Years – A personal photographic documentary

23. Must see places in USA and Japan - A kaleidoscopic photographic documentary

24. Grandeurs of the World - A kaleidoscopic photographic documentary

25. Corneliu Leu – writer on the same wavelength as Mark Twain. An American viewpoint

26. From Berkeley to Pompeii via Rome – A kaleidoscopic photographic documentary

27. From America to Europe via Japan - A kaleidoscopic photographic documentary

28. Discover America and Japan - A photographic documentary

29. J. R. Lucas – philosopher on a creative parallel with Plato, An American viewpoint

30. From America to Switzerland via France - A photographic documentary

31. From Bretton Woods to New York via Cape Cod - A photographic documentary

32. Splendid Places on the Atlantic Coast of the U. S. A. - A photographic documentary

33. Fourteen nice Cities on three Continents - A photographic documentary

34. 17 Picturesque Cities on the World Map - A photographic documentary

35. Unforgettable Places from Four Continents, including Trump buildings - A photographic documentary

36. Dediu Newsletter, Volume 1, Number 1, 6 December 2016 – Monthly news, review, comments and suggestions for a better and wiser world

37. Dediu Newsletter, Volume 1, Number 2, 6 January 2017 (available also at www.derc.com).

38. Dediu Newsletter, Volume 1, Number 3, 6 February 2017 (available at www.derc.com).

39. London and Greenwich, - A photographic documentary

40. Dediu Newsletter, Volume 1, Number 4, 6 March 2017 (available also at www.derc.com).

41. Dediu Newsletter, Volume 1, Number 5, 6 April 2017 (available also at www.derc.com).

42. Dediu Newsletter, Volume 1, Number 6, 6 May 2017 (available also at www.derc.com).

43. Dediu Newsletter, Volume 1, Number 7, 6 June 2017 (available also at www.derc.com).

44. London, Oxford and Cambridge, A photographic documentary

45. Dediu Newsletter, Volume 1, Number 8, 6 July 2017 (available also at www.derc.com).

46. Dediu Newsletter, Volume 1, Number 9, 6 August 2017 (available also at www.derc.com).

47. Dediu Newsletter, Volume 1, Number 10, 6 September 2017 (available also at www.derc.com).

48. Three Great Professors: President Woodrow Wilson, Historian German Arciniegas, and Mathematician Gheorghe Vranceanu – A chronological and photographic documentary

49. Dediu Newsletter, Volume 1, Number 11, 6 October 2017 (available also at www.derc.com).

50. Dediu Newsletter, Volume 1, Number 12, 6 November 2017 (available also at www.derc.com).

51. Dediu Newsletter, Volume 2, Number 1 (13), 6 December 2017 (available also at www.derc.com).

52. Two Great Leaders: Augustus and George Washington - A chronological and photographic documentary

53. Dediu Newsletter, Volume 2, Number 2 (14), 6 January 2018 (available also at www.derc.com).

54. Newton, Benjamin Franklin, and Gauss, A chronological and photographic documentary

55. Dediu Newsletter, Volume 2, Number 3 (15), 6 February 2018 (available also at www.derc.com).

56. 2017: World Top Events, But Many Little Known, A chronological and photographic documentary

57. Dediu Newsletter, Volume 2, Number 4 (16), 6 March 2018 (available also at www.derc.com).

58. Vergilius, Horatius, Ovidius, and Shakespeare - A chronological and photographic documentary.

59. Dediu Newsletter, Volume 2, Number 5 (17), 6 April 2018 (available also at www.derc.com).

60. Dediu Newsletter, Volume 2, Number 6 (18), 6 May 2018 (available also at www.derc.com).

61. Vivaldi, Bach, Mozart, and Verdi - A chronological and photographic documentary.

62. Dediu Newsletter, Volume 2, Number 7 (19), 6 June 2018 (available also at www.derc.com).

63. Dediu Newsletter, Volume 2, Number 8 (20), 6 July 2018 (available also at www.derc.com).

64. Dediu Newsletter, Volume 2, Number 9 (21), 6 August 2018 (available also at www.derc.com).

65. World History, a new perspective - A chronological and photographic documentary.

66. World Humor History with over 100 Jokes, a new perspective - A chronological and photographic documentary

67. Dediu Newsletter, Volume 2, Number 10 (22), 6 September 2018 (available also at www.derc.com).

68. Dediu Newsletter, Volume 2, Number 11 (23), 6 October 2018 (available also at www.derc.com).

69. Dediu Newsletter, Volume 2, Number 12 (24), 6 November 2018

70. Da Vinci, Michelangelo, Rembrandt, Rodin - A chronological and photographic documentary

71. Dediu Newsletter, Volume 3, Number 1 (25), 6 December 2018

72. Dediu Newsletter, Volume 3, Number 2 (26), 6 January 2019

73. From Euclid to Edison – revelries in the past 75 years - A chronological and photographic documentary

74. – Socrates to Churchill Aphorisms celebrated after 1960 - A chronological and photographic documentary

75. - Dediu Newsletter, Volume 3, Number 3 (27), 6 February 2019

76. – Hippocrates to Fleming: Medicine History celebrated after 1943 - A chronological and photographic documentary

77. - Dediu Newsletter, Volume 3, Number 4 (28), 6 March 2019

78. - Dediu Newsletter, Volume 3, Number 5 (29), 6 April 2019

79 – Archimedes to Ford: Invention History celebrated after 1943 - A chronological and photographic documentary

80 - Dediu Newsletter, Volume 3, Number 6 (30), 6 May 2019

81 – Sutherland to Pavarotti: Great Singers History - A chronological and photographic documentary

82 - Dediu Newsletter, Volume 3, Number 7 (31), 6 June 2019

83 - Dediu Newsletter, Volume 3, Number 8 (32), 6 July 2019

84 – Augustus to Rockefeller: History of the Wealthiest People - A chronological and photographic documentary

85 - Dediu Newsletter, Volume 3, Number 9 (33), 6 August 2019

86 – Pythagoras to Fermi: History of Science - A chronological and photographic documentary

87 - Dediu Newsletter, Volume 3, Number 10 (34), 6 September 2019

88 – Our Future is Sustainable Peace and Prosperity – Moving from conflicts to harmony and peace

89 - Dediu Newsletter, Volume 3, Number 11 (35), 6 October 2019 – World Monthly Report with news

90 – Our Future Depends on Good World Educations – Moving from frail education to solid education

91 - Dediu Newsletter, Volume 3, Number 12 (36), 6 November 2019 – World Monthly Report with News and Suggestions for Sustainable Peace, Freedom and Prosperity

92 – Friendly, Helpful & Smart World Management - Moving from bureaucracy to responsive world management

93 – If You Want Peace, Prepare for Peace! – Moving from preparation for war to preparation for peace

94 - Dediu Newsletter, Volume 4, Number 1 (37), 6 December 2019 – World Monthly Report with News and Suggestions for Sustainable Peace, Freedom and Prosperity

95 – World with One Country & its Ten Friendly Regions - Moving from 195 disagreeing countries, to 1 country with 10 collaborating regions

96 - Dediu Newsletter, Volume 4, Number 2 (38), 6 January 2020 – World Monthly Report with News and Suggestions for Sustainable Peace, Freedom and Prosperity

97 – After 10,000 Years of Conflicts, People want 10,000 Years of Harmony - Moving from continuous wars to stable peace

98 - Dediu Newsletter, Volume 4, Number 3 (39), 6 February 2020 – World Monthly Report with News and Suggestions for Sustainable Peace, Freedom and Prosperity

99 - Dediu Newsletter, Volume 4, Number 4 (40), 6 March 2020 – World Monthly Report with News and Suggestions for Sustainable Peace, Freedom and Prosperity

100 - Dediu Newsletter, Volume 4, Number 5 (41), 6 April 2020 – World Monthly Report

Mathematical and technical research papers published in international mathematical and technical journals

1. Dediu, M. On the lens spaces. *Rev. Roumaine Math. Pures Appl.* **14** (1969) 623-627.

2. Dediu, M. Sur quelques propriétés des espaces lenticulaires. (French) *Rev. Roumaine Math. Pures Appl.* **17** (1972), 871-874.

3. Vranceanu, G; Dediu, M. Tangent vector fields in projective spaces V_3 and in the lens spaces $L^3(3)$. (Romanian) Stud. Cerc. Mat. **24** (1972), 1585-1600.

4. Dediu, M. Tangent vector fields on lens spaces of dimension three (Italian) *Atti Accad. Naz. Lincei Rend. Cl. Sci. Fis. Mat. Natur.* **54** (1974), no. 2, 329-334 (1977

5. Dediu, M. Campi di vettori tangenti sullo spazio lenticolare $L^7(3)$. (Italian) *Atti Accad. Naz. Lincei Rend. Cl. Sci. Fis. Mat. Natur. (8)* **58** (1975), no. 1, 14-17.

6. Dediu, M. Tre campi di vettori tangenti indepedenti sugli spazi lenticolari di dimensione $4n+3$. (Italian) *Atti Accad. Naz. Lincei Rend. Cl. Sci. Fis. Mat. Natur. (8)* **58** (1975), no. 2, 174-178.

7. Dediu, M. Sopra la metrica Vranceanu generalizzata (Italian) *Atti Accad. Naz. Lincei Rend. Cl. Sci. Fis. Mat. Natur. (8)* **58** (1975), no.3, 354-359).

8. Dediu, S.; Dediu, M. Sopra gli spazi proiettivi. *Rend. Sem. Fac. Sci. Univ. Cagliari* **46** (1976), suppl., 149-152.

9. Dediu, M.; Caddeo, Renzo; Dediu Sofia Alcune proprietà di una superficie immersa in uno spazio di Hilbert. (Italian) *Rend. Ist. Mat. Univ. Trieste* **8** (1976), no. 2, 147-161 (1977)

10. Dediu, S.; Dediu, M.; Caddeo, R. Alcune proprietà della metrica di Vranceanu generalizzata. (Italian) *Rend Sem. Fac. Sci. Univ Cagliari* **46** (1976), suppl., 153-161.

11. Dediu, Sofia; Dediu, M.; Caddeo, Renzo The Vrănceanu metric in local coordinates. (Italian) *Atti Accad. Sci. Lett. Arti Palermo Parte I (4)* **37** (1977/78). 331-339 (1980).

12. Dediu, M.; Caddeo, Renzo; Dediu, Sofia The extension of an *E*-premanifold to an *E*-manifold. (Italian) *Rend. Circ. Mat. Palermo (2)* **27** (1978), no. 3, 353-358.

13. Dediu, Michael M. Nutshell Plus - the relational file manager (version 1.0) *(Academic Journal) Computer.* June 1988, Vol. **21,** Issue 6, p 96.

14. Dediu, Michael M. Hot Line electronic phone book *(Academic Journal) Computer* June 1988, Vol. **21**, Issue 6, p 97.

15. Dediu, Michael M. A VMS-based calendar and notification software *(Academic Journal) Computer* Dec 1988, Vol. **21,** Issue 12, p 84.

16. Dediu, Michael M. Visual Cobol-85 for MS-DOS *(Academic Journal) Computer* Dec 1988, Vol. **21,** Issue 12, p 85.

17. Dediu, Michael M. GoldWorks AXLE - a learning tool for developing expert systems *(Academic Journal) Computer* Jan 1989, Vol. **22,** Issue 1, p113.

18. Dediu, Michael M. ALS Prolog - a professional compiler for MS-DOS computers *(Academic Journal) Computer* Jan 1989, Vol. **22**, Issue 1, p 113-114.

19. Dediu, Michael M. ILS powerful software for signal processing *(Academic Journal) Computer* March 1989, Vol. **22**, Issue 3, p 85-87.

Mathematical Reviews: American Mathematical Society sent for review, over the years, 287 mathematical research papers and books, to Michael M. Dediu, and his reviews where published in the Mathematical Reviews of the AMS.

Michael M. Dediu is the editor of these books (also on Amazon.com, and www.derc.com):

1. Sophia Dediu: The life and its torrents – Ana. In Europe around 1920
2. Proceedings of the 4th International Conference "Advanced Composite Materials Engineering" COMAT 2012
3. Adolf Shvedchikov: I am an eternal child of spring – poems in English, Italian, French, German, Spanish and Russian
4. Adolf Shvedchikov: Life's Enigma – poems in English, Italian and Russian
5. Adolf Shvedchikov: Everyone wants to be HAPPY – poems in English, Spanish and Russian
6. Adolf Shvedchikov: My Life, My Love – poems in English, Italian and Russian
7. Adolf Shvedchikov: I am the gardener of love – poems in English and Russian
8. Adolf Shvedchikov: Amaretta di Saronno – poems in English and Russian
9. Adolf Shvedchikov: A Russian Rediscovers America
10. Adolf Shvedchikov: Parade of Life - poems in English and Russian
11. Adolf Shvedchikov: Overcoming Sorrow - poems in English and Russian
12. Sophia Dediu: Sophia meets Japan
13. Corneliu Leu: Roosevelt, Churchill, Stalin and Hitler: Their surprising role in Eastern Europe in 1944
14. Proceedings of the 5th International Conference "Computational Mechanics and Virtual Engineering" COMEC 2013
15. Georgeta Simion – Potanga: Beyond Imagination: A Thought-provoking novel inspired from mid-20th century events
16. Ana Dediu: The poetry of my life in Europe and the USA
17. Ana Dediu: The Four Graces
18. Proceedings of the 5th International Conference "Advanced Composite Materials Engineering" COMAT 2014
19. Sophia Dediu: Chocolate Cook Book: Is there such a thing as too much chocolate?

20. Sorin Vlase: Mechanical Identifiability in Automotive Engineering

21. Gabriel Dima: The Evolution of the Aerostructures – Concept and Technologies

22. Proceedings of the 6th International Conference "Computational Mechanics and Virtual Engineering" COMEC 2015

23. Sophia Dediu: Cook Book 1 A-B-C Common sense cooking

24. Sophia Dediu: Dim Sum Spring Festival

25. Ana Dediu and Sophia Dediu: Europe in 1985: A chronological and photographic documentary

26. Stefan Staretu: Europe: Serbian Despotate of Srem and the Romanian Area – Between the 14th and the 16th Centuries

Paris - L'Opéra de Paris (or L'Académie Nationale de Musique, or l'Opéra Garnier, or Le Palais Garnier, or L'Opéra), a 1,979-seat opera house, built from 1861 to 1875, now mainly used for ballet.

Auspicium Melioris Aevi (Hope of a better age)